FRUGAL COOKING

WITH YOUR

INSTANT POT®

FRUGAL COOKING

 WITH YOUR
INSTANT POT®

Delicious, Fuss-Free Meals That Cost
$3 or Less per Serving

Drew Maresco

Author of *3-Step Slow Cooker Cookbook*

with Dallyn Maresco

PAGE STREET
PUBLISHING CO

PAGE STREET
PUBLISHING CO.

First published in 2020 by
Page Street Publishing Co.
27 Congress Street, Suite 105
Salem, MA 01970
www.pagestreetpublishing.com

Distributed by Macmillan, sales in Canada by The Canadian Manda Group.

24 23 22 21 20   1 2 3 4 5

ISBN-13: 978-1-64567-178-7
ISBN-10: 1-64567-178-X

Library of Congress Control Number: 2019957334

Cover and book design by Molly Gillespie for Page Street Publishing Co.
Photography by Toni Zernik

Printed and bound in the United States

Instant Pot® is a registered trademark of Double Insight, Inc., which was not involved in the creation of this book.

Note: Prices throughout this book are estimates based on the cost of ingredients at the time of this book's production. Prices may vary depending on time and place of purchase.

This book is dedicated to
everyone who's looking for
fast, affordable and nutritious
meals to feed their family.

CONTENTS

Introduction

What do you do when you get home from work after a long day and nothing sounds better than a delicious pot roast? Before the Instant Pot, this was all but impossible, but now you can make that roast in under an hour. Sure, pressure cookers have been around for ages, but the intimidation that came with learning how to use them was overwhelming, plus, we've all heard the scary stories that revolved around them, which kept most of us from ever using them (or using them again). Thanks to the Instant Pot, with its safety features alone, those are no longer concerns to worry about. It's no wonder people jumped on the bandwagon to get one and try it out for themselves. So, indeed, the Instant Pot and multifunction pressure cookers are the new kitchen game changers.

Admittedly, I was very late to the Instant Pot party. It's not because it seemed like a bad kitchen item to have; I just tend to be a bit skeptical anytime a new appliance comes out that promises to be the kitchen time-saver of the century. Although the Instant Pot was a new concept, pressure cooking, as I mentioned earlier, has been around for years. Could an all-in-one appliance really make pressure cooking a popular technique again? If I'm going to be completely honest, I was convinced it was just a fad, and I didn't give it much thought. Once a few friends of mine bought their own Instant Pots, I started getting asked whether I had one or had any recipes for it, which I didn't at the time. What I found incredibly interesting, though, was their excitement as they'd talk about it, what meals they made and how easy it was to use. They continued to use it and couldn't get enough of its ease of use and the time saving that came with having it in their kitchen. So, I finally caved—I bought my own! And the appeal of this appliance is real.

The main goal when I write a cookbook, or really any recipe, is to get everyone excited about cooking. I want to show you that you don't have to break the bank or follow complicated steps to make a great-tasting meal. I believe making your own food should feel empowering. Why? Because you have the power of choice. You choose what you want to eat, what ingredients you're going to use, what brands you want and whether you make that recipe again. And if the Instant Pot, all on its own, can get people excited about making their own meals, this is something that's worth exploring.

With all of that said, after writing my last book, the *3-Step Slow Cooker Cookbook*, I felt it was a must to do an Instant Pot book next! It's because these two kitchen appliances have home cooks everywhere feeling like heroes in their own kitchens! They give everyone the ability to make great-tasting meals, even on the busiest weekdays. And it's that kind of feeling that gets people excited about cooking and removes a lot of the intimidation that surrounds home cooking.

Another thing I am excited about with this book is that it comes with a timely topic: staying budget-minded—keeping your wallet and your stomach full. There's a common misbelief that take-out is cheaper than making food at home. Well, with the recipes in this book, you will be assured that you are saving money on your dinners and giving your family the healthier options! My goal with this book is to challenge the belief that eating out is more affordable. How so? By packing this book with delicious meals that come in at $3 or less per serving and cook in just four steps or less, making them that much easier. Take that, fast-food restaurants!

My hope is that this book becomes your main resource for budget-friendly meals. Using fresh ingredients and avoiding big-name brands to keep costs low, our focus is to make every recipe easy on the grocery bill. Using the cheapest cuts of meat and buying vegetables in large quantities guarantees you the most cost-effective buying options out there. These recipes are all very straightforward and approachable for anyone, whether it's a new recipe you have never heard of or one that you adore made in a fresh new way, you'll love how delicious and easy they all are. And if you're like me, once you find those recipes that really resonate with you, you will make them again and again. Because they're so straightforward, I encourage you to make them as written, then next time you prepare them, try adjusting them to your preferences—turning them into your own! That's the best way to become a better cook! And to learn how to cook the things that you and your family enjoy. I definitely recommend it!

Drew Maresco

The Golden Rules of Using Your Instant Pot

- Don't dirty a second pan; use the sauté mode! It's there for a reason. After cooking, set it to sauté and use the pan drippings to make a delicious sauce. This mode is perfect for both before and after pressure cooking.

- Always make sure your lid is clean and the seal ring is secure. Your pot won't come to pressure if the seal ring is not in place properly.

- Such things as pasta, rice, beans and grains will expand, so be careful not to overfill the pot.

- Add thickeners at the end of cooking. Adding them at the beginning can cause your food to burn or cause the liquid to come out of the venting knob.

- Never put the pot under pressure unless there is at least 1 cup (240 ml) of liquid in the pot. Without it, the pot won't come to pressure, and you risk damaging the device.

- After sautéing meats, add your liquid and deglaze the brown bits on the bottom. This keeps the pot from burning your food and it gets that great flavor into your meal.

- Dairy tends to break when under pressure. To ensure your meal is exactly what you want it to be, mix in your cheese, milk and cream at the end.

Everyday Comforts

Comfort foods come in a variety of forms. For some people, it's a slow-cooked roast that's fork-tender; for others, it may be a spicy bowl of chicken jambalaya (page 45) or even a sticky pulled pork (page 37). To say we all think different things taste like home is an understatement. That's what this chapter explores, diving deep into every meaning of the term comfort, with classics you'll recognize and others that just might be a first for you to try! Every recipe is a unique take on the original with some exciting and budget-friendly adjustments, such as using cheaper cuts of meat and serving sides like potatoes or noodles. These dishes are sure to satisfy!

Seasoned Pork Tenderloin with Gravy

A savory and flavorful pork tenderloin all cooked together in one pot. Nothing goes to waste: Its pan juices make for a delicious gravy that can be poured over the pork or mashed potatoes.

Serves 6

$1.07 per serving

1½ lb (680 g) pork tenderloin, cut into 2 pieces

2 tsp (12 g) salt

1 tsp freshly ground black pepper

1 tbsp (8 g) chili powder

1 tsp onion powder

1 tsp garlic powder

1 tbsp (15 ml) canola oil

1 (14.5-oz [429-ml]) can chicken broth

2 tbsp (16 g) cornstarch mixed with 2 tbsp (30 ml) water

Mashed potatoes, for serving (optional)

Season the pork with the salt, pepper, chili powder, onion powder and garlic powder. Turn the pot to sauté mode on HIGH until the screen says hot. Add the oil. Add the pork and cook for 2 to 3 minutes per side. Add the broth. Turn the pot to HIGH pressure, secure the lid, adjust the valve to sealing and set the timer for 15 minutes. When the time is up, do a quick release by turning the valve to venting. Once finished, release the lid.

Remove the pork from the pot. Stir in the cornstarch mixture until thickened. Serve the pork with the gravy on top alongside mashed potatoes (if using).

Puerto Rican Chicken with Sofrito Rice

This chicken and rice dish is one that you may not be familiar with, but might be one that you will want to add to your recipe rotation. A wonderful pairing of tender chicken thighs with a Puerto Rican–spiced rice that's flavor-packed and vibrantly colored. Finished with fresh lime and cilantro, this dinner will not disappoint!

Serves 6

$2.06 per serving

1 tsp ground cumin
¾ tsp paprika
½ tsp chili powder
½ tsp cayenne pepper
½ tsp onion powder
½ tsp garlic powder
¼ tsp ground coriander
½ tsp salt
¼ tsp freshly ground black pepper
1½ lbs (680 g) boneless, skinless chicken thighs
2 tbsp (30 ml) canola oil

Sofrito Rice

2 tbsp (30 ml) canola oil
3 cloves garlic, minced
1 small green bell pepper, seeded and diced
1 medium-sized onion, diced
1 jalapeño pepper, seeded and diced
¼ cup (10 g) fresh cilantro, finely chopped, plus more for serving
¼ tsp ground coriander
¼ tsp ground cumin
¼ tsp ground turmeric
¼ tsp garlic powder
¼ tsp oregano
¼ tsp salt
¼ tsp freshly ground black pepper
1 (15-oz [444-ml]) can tomato sauce
1¼ cups (295 ml) water
⅔ cup (86 g) frozen peas, rinsed
1 cup (195 g) uncooked basmati rice

1 lime, cut into wedges, for serving

In a small bowl, stir together the cumin, paprika, chili powder, cayenne, onion powder, garlic powder, coriander, salt and black pepper. Toss the chicken in the seasoning mixture. Turn the pot to sauté mode on HIGH until the screen says hot. Add the oil, then the chicken, working in batches if necessary, and cook for 3 to 4 minutes per side, or until browned. Remove from the pot and set aside.

Prepare the sofrito rice: Add the oil, then the garlic, bell pepper, onion, jalapeño and cilantro to the pot and cook for 2 to 3 minutes. Stir in the coriander, cumin, turmeric, garlic powder, oregano, salt and black pepper, cooking for 1 minute. Stir in the tomato sauce, water and peas. Return the chicken to the pot. Pour the rice on top. Turn the pot to HIGH pressure, secure the lid, adjust the valve to sealing and set the timer for 8 minutes. When the time is up, do a quick release by turning the valve to venting. Once finished, release the lid.

Serve topped with cilantro and a lime wedge for squeezing.

Balsamic Roast Beef and Potatoes

This fork-tender roast beef and potato dish comes together with easy prep and is a full meal in one pot. This quintessential American comfort food, with its mouthwatering balsamic richness, is sure to surprise and delight.

Serves 6

$2.85 per serving

3 lb (1.4 kg) beef chuck roast

2 tsp (12 g) salt, plus more to taste

1 tsp freshly ground black pepper, plus more to taste

2 tbsp (30 ml) canola oil, divided

1 large onion, sliced

4 cloves garlic, minced

¾ cup (175 ml) beef broth

¼ cup (60 ml) balsamic vinegar

1 tbsp (15 ml) Worcestershire sauce

1 tbsp (15 ml) soy sauce

1 tbsp (15 g) light brown sugar

3 lbs (1.4 kg) russet potatoes, peeled and quartered

½ cup (112 g/1 stick) unsalted butter

⅓ cup (80 ml) milk

Pat the roast dry and season with the salt and pepper. Turn the pot to sauté mode on HIGH until the screen says hot. Add 1 tablespoon (15 ml) of the oil, then the beef, and cook for 4 minutes per side, or until browned. Remove from the pot and set aside.

Add the remaining tablespoon (15 ml) of oil and the onion to the pot and cook for 10 to 12 minutes, or until browned. Add the garlic and cook for 1 to 2 minutes. In a small bowl, stir together the beef broth, balsamic, Worcestershire, soy sauce and brown sugar until the sugar dissolves. Return the roast to the pot and pour in the sauce.

Place the tall egg rack in the pot so that it rests above the meat mixture. Place the handled steamer pan on top of the rack and place the potatoes on top. Turn the pot to HIGH pressure, secure the lid, adjust the valve to sealing and set the timer for 45 minutes. When the time is up, do a quick release by turning the valve to venting. Once finished, release the lid.

Remove the potatoes from the pot. In a large bowl, mash together the potatoes and butter. Gradually add the milk and season with salt and pepper to taste. Serve the beef with the pan juices and onion mixture alongside the mashed potatoes.

Note: If you do not have the handled steamer pan and the tall egg rack, you can cook the potatoes on the stovetop by boiling them in salted water for 20 minutes, until fork-tender.

Whole Roasted Chicken and Potatoes

Who doesn't love a roasted chicken? Buying chicken whole gives you the best bang for your buck, while the Instant Pot will give you tender and juicy meat. But it's the spice rub that really packs in the flavor here. Just pop it under the broiler for a few minutes at the end to crisp the skin, and dinner is ready with minimal effort.

Serves 4

$1.93 per serving

1 (4½-lb [2-kg]) chicken

2 tsp (12 g) salt

1 tsp freshly ground black pepper

2 tsp (5 g) paprika

1 tsp dried oregano

1 tsp onion powder

½ tsp garlic powder

2 tsp (2 g) dried thyme

½ tsp cayenne pepper

2 lbs (905 g) red-skinned potatoes, quartered

1 (14.5-oz [429-ml]) can chicken broth

Remove the skin from the chicken if not broiling after cooking.

In a small bowl, stir together the salt, pepper, paprika, oregano, onion powder, garlic powder, thyme and cayenne. Using your hands, rub the chicken with the seasonings, making sure to get it everywhere. In the pot, combine the potatoes and broth. Place the chicken in the pot on top of the potatoes. Turn the pot to HIGH pressure, secure the lid, adjust the valve to sealing and set the timer for 30 minutes. When the time is up, do a quick release by turning the valve to venting. Once finished, release the lid.

Carefully remove the chicken from the pot and place on a parchment-lined rimmed baking sheet. If you wish to broil the chicken, set the oven to broil on HIGH. Broil the chicken for 5 to 10 minutes, or until the skin is crispy.

Meanwhile, remove the potatoes from the pot and discard the cooking liquid. Serve the chicken with the potatoes.

Cheesy Chicken and Rice

All the best things about a casserole come together even faster in this comfort food classic. Rice is a cheap and filling ingredient, that when combined with chicken, veggies and cheese, makes a great dinner for the whole family. Even the pickiest eaters will love it.

Serves 6

$2.18 **per serving**

2 lbs (905 g) boneless, skinless chicken thighs, cut into ½" (1.3-cm) pieces

2 tsp (12 g) salt

1 tsp freshly ground black pepper

2 tbsp (30 ml) canola oil

1 medium-sized onion, chopped

2 carrots, chopped

2 celery ribs, chopped

4 cloves garlic, minced

4 cups (946 ml) chicken broth

2 cups (390 g) uncooked basmati rice

1 cup (115 g) shredded medium Cheddar cheese

⅓ cup (20 g) fresh parsley, finely chopped, for garnish

Season the chicken with the salt and pepper. Turn the pot to sauté mode on HIGH until the screen says hot. Add the oil, then the chicken, and cook for 3 to 4 minutes, or until browned on all sides. Add the onion, carrots, celery and garlic, and cook for 5 to 7 minutes, or until softened and translucent. Stir in the broth. Pour the rice on top.

Turn the pot to HIGH pressure, secure the lid, adjust the valve to sealing and set the timer for 10 minutes. When the time is up, do a quick release by turning the valve to venting. Once finished, release the lid.

Stir in the cheese until fully melted. Serve topped with the parsley.

Creamy Garlic Chicken

Creamy, garlicky and served over rice. This simple chicken dinner comes together in just minutes and is as delicious as it is cost effective, due to its short ingredient list. Truly a quick-fix meal.

Serves 6

$1.92 per serving

1½ lbs (680 g) boneless, skinless chicken thighs

2 tsp (12 g) salt

1 tsp freshly ground black pepper

2 tbsp (30 ml) canola oil

1 medium-sized onion, diced

8 cloves garlic, minced

1½ cups (355 ml) chicken broth

1½ cups (293 g) uncooked basmati rice

½ cup (120 ml) half-and-half

2 tbsp (16 g) cornstarch mixed with 2 tbsp (30 ml) water

Season the chicken with the salt and pepper. Turn the pot to sauté mode on HIGH until the screen says hot. Add the oil, then the chicken, and cook for 2 to 3 minutes per side, or until the chicken starts to brown. Remove from the pot and set aside.

Add the onion to the pot and cook for 10 to 12 minutes, until just browning. Add the garlic and stir for 1 minute. Stir in the broth and return the chicken to the pot. Turn the pot to HIGH pressure, secure the lid, adjust the valve to sealing and set the timer for 10 minutes. When the time is up, do a quick release by turning the valve to venting. Once finished, release the lid.

Meanwhile, cook the rice according to the package directions.

Remove the chicken from the pot. Stir the half-and-half into the pot, then the cornstarch mixture until thickened. Serve with the garlic cream sauce on top of the chicken and with rice.

Bourbon-Glazed Chicken and Rice

This sweet and tangy bourbon glaze is easily the showstopper in this meal. It takes little effort to make something that truly captures so much flavor. Serving this over rice or with vegetables makes for a perfect weeknight dinner.

Serves 6

$2.29 per serving

1½ lbs (680 g) boneless, skinless chicken thighs

1 tsp salt

¾ tsp freshly ground black pepper, divided

2 tbsp (30 ml) canola oil

½ cup (120 ml) bourbon or whiskey

½ cup (170 g) honey

½ cup (120 ml) apple juice

2 cloves garlic, minced

½ cup (120 ml) low-sodium soy sauce

¼ cup (60 ml) cider vinegar

½ tsp ground ginger

1½ cups (293 g) uncooked basmati rice

Season the chicken with the salt and ½ teaspoon of the pepper. Turn the pot to sauté mode on HIGH until the screen says hot. Add the oil, then the chicken, and cook for 3 to 4 minutes per side, or until browned. In a small bowl, stir together the bourbon, honey, apple juice, garlic, soy sauce, vinegar, remaining ¼ teaspoon of pepper and ginger. Add the sauce to the pot. Turn the pot to HIGH pressure, secure the lid, adjust the valve to sealing and set the timer for 15 minutes. When the time is up, do a quick release by turning the valve to venting. Once finished, release the lid.

Meanwhile, cook the rice according to the package directions.

Remove the chicken from the pot and set aside. Turn the pot to sauté mode on HIGH. Cook the sauce for 6 to 8 minutes, until the sauce is reduced by half. Serve over the chicken with the rice.

Cheeseburger Sloppy Joes

We didn't want to mess with a burger because frankly, is there really room for improvement there? We've combined our favorite things about the already budget-friendly sloppy joe and a classic cheeseburger to make this a hybrid meal that tastes great and is even easier to make.

Serves 8

$1.76 per serving

2 lbs (905 g) ground beef

1 tsp salt

½ tsp freshly ground black pepper

1 medium-sized onion, diced

3 cloves garlic, minced

2 tsp (5 g) paprika

2 tbsp (32 g) tomato paste

1 tbsp (15 ml) Worcestershire sauce

1 cup (240 ml) beef broth

1 cup (240 ml) tomato sauce

¼ cup (32 g) cornstarch mixed with ¼ cup (60 ml) water

1 cup (115 g) shredded Cheddar cheese

8 hamburger buns

Optional Toppings

Pickles

Mustard

Ketchup

Cooked bacon

Cheese slices

Turn the pot to sauté mode on HIGH until the screen says hot. Add the beef, salt and pepper, and cook for 5 to 7 minutes, or until no longer pink. Drain any accumulated grease and liquid. Add the onion and cook for 2 to 3 minutes, then add the garlic and cook for 1 minute. Stir in the paprika, tomato paste and Worcestershire until combined. Stir in the broth and tomato sauce. Turn the pot to HIGH pressure, secure the lid, adjust the valve to sealing and set the timer for 10 minutes. When the time is up, do a quick release by turning the valve to venting. Once finished, release the lid.

Stir in the cornstarch mixture until thickened. Stir in the cheese until just melted. Let sit for 10 minutes. Serve on hamburger buns topped with your choice of toppings.

Salisbury Steak Meatloaf

Salisbury steak is known for its delicious caramelized onion gravy. Combining that with a classic meatloaf makes for an easy, flavor-packed, more affordable dinner that's fit for a crowd. Serve along with mashed potatoes for the perfect meat and potatoes dinner.

Serves 6

$1.97 per serving

¼ cup (60 ml) canola oil

2 large onions, diced

2 tsp (5 g) onion powder, divided

2 tbsp (30 ml) Worcestershire sauce

1 (14.5-oz [429-ml]) can beef broth

2 lbs (905 g) ground beef

2 large eggs

1 cup (110 g) breadcrumbs

1½ tsp (9 g) salt

½ tsp freshly ground black pepper

1 tsp garlic powder

3 tbsp (24 g) cornstarch mixed with 3 tbsp (45 ml) water

Mashed potatoes, for serving (optional)

Turn the pot to sauté mode on HIGH until the screen says hot. Add the oil, then the onions, and cook for 10 to 15 minutes, or until browned and starting to caramelize. Remove about ¼ cup (40 g) of the onions. Stir 1 teaspoon of the onion powder as well as the Worcestershire and broth into the pot. Turn off the pot.

In a large bowl, using your hands, combine the beef, eggs, breadcrumbs, salt, pepper, remaining teaspoon of onion powder, reserved onion and garlic powder until well combined. Shape the meat mixture into a round loaf and place it in the handled steamer pan. Add the tall egg rack to the pot and place the handled steamer pan on top. Turn the pot to HIGH pressure, secure the lid, adjust the valve to sealing and set the timer for 35 minutes. When the time is up, do a quick release by turning the valve to venting. Once finished, release the lid.

Remove the pan and rack from the pot. Stir in the cornstarch mixture until thickened. Serve the meatloaf sliced with the gravy over the top and with mashed potatoes (if using).

Note: If you do not have the handled steamer pan and the tall egg rack, you can use the trivet that comes with your Instant Pot and line it with parchment paper to ensure your meatloaf doesn't fall apart.

Potatoes with Country Sausage Gravy

A delicious cross between biscuits and gravy and a potato hash, this country breakfast-turned-dinner will have everyone feeling satisfied. The flavorful sausage and prepared hash browns make this filling without having to break the bank.

Serves 6

$2.12 per serving

1 (2-lb [905-g]) package cubed hash browns

2 tbsp (30 ml) canola oil

2 lbs (905 g) ground Italian sausage

1 tsp salt

1 tsp freshly ground black pepper

1 large onion, diced

4 cloves garlic

8 oz (225 g) baby bella mushrooms, quartered

1 (14.5-oz [429-ml]) can chicken broth

½ tsp dried thyme

1 cup (240 ml) heavy cream

Cook the hash browns in the oven according to the package directions.

Turn the pot to sauté mode on HIGH until the screen says hot. Add the oil, then the sausage, salt and pepper, and cook for 4 to 5 minutes, or until no longer pink. Add the onion and garlic, and cook for 3 to 5 minutes. Add the mushrooms and cook for 5 to 7 minutes. Stir in the broth and thyme. Turn the pot to HIGH pressure, secure the lid, adjust the valve to sealing and set the timer for 8 minutes. When the time is up, do a quick release by turning the valve to venting. Once finished, release the lid.

Turn the pot to sauté mode on HIGH. Cook for 7 to 10 minutes, or until the liquid has reduced by half. Stir in the cream and serve over the hash browns.

Orange-Balsamic Pork Roast

Orange and balsamic are a delicious pairing that accompanies this pork roast perfectly. The fresh rosemary lends a citrusy-pine flavor to the orange and balsamic glaze, keeping the number of ingredients low with flavors that pack a punch. This meal will impress!

Serves 8

$1.79 **per serving**

2 tsp (12 g) salt

1 tsp freshly ground black pepper

Zest and juice of 2 large oranges

¼ cup (60 ml) + 2 tbsp (30 ml) canola oil, divided

¼ cup (60 ml) balsamic vinegar

¼ cup (60 ml) molasses

2 tbsp (4 g) chopped fresh rosemary

3 lb (1.4 kg) pork roast, cut into 2 pieces

1½ cups (355 ml) water

In a large bowl, stir together the salt, pepper, orange zest and juice, ¼ cup (60 ml) of the oil, balsamic, molasses and rosemary. Submerge the pork and marinate for 1 hour in the refrigerator.

Turn the pot to sauté mode on HIGH until the screen says hot. Add the remaining 2 tablespoons (30 ml) of oil, then the pork (reserve the marinade), and cook for 3 to 4 minutes per side, or until browned on all sides. Remove from the pot and place on the trivet. Add the water to the pot and insert the pork on its trivet. Turn the pot to HIGH pressure, secure the lid, adjust the valve to sealing and set the timer for 40 minutes. When the time is up, do a quick release by turning the valve to venting. Once finished, release the lid.

Meanwhile, in a small pan over medium heat, cook the reserved marinade for 10 minutes, or until reduced by half.

Serve the pork with the glaze poured over the top.

Savory Apple Pork Tenderloin

Apples are one of the most common pairings with pork. The tenderloin and apples help cut costs, making this rendition new and exciting by pairing them both with caramelized onions and bacon. This makes for a savory, almost chutney-like sauce that's just so darn good, you won't be able to get enough of it; I promise you'll be hooked on your first bite.

Serves 6

$2.42 per serving

10 slices bacon, diced

1 large onion, diced

2 cloves garlic, minced

¼ tsp dried thyme

½ tsp dried parsley

1½ tsp (9 g) salt, divided

¾ tsp freshly ground black pepper, divided

2 lb (905 g) pork tenderloin, cut into 2 pieces

2 tbsp (30 ml) canola oil

1 cup (240 ml) apple juice

1 apple, cored and diced

1 tbsp (8 g) cornstarch mixed with 1 tbsp (15 ml) water

Turn the pot to sauté mode on HIGH until the screen says hot. Add the bacon and cook for 15 minutes, until the bacon is crispy. Add the onion and cook for 5 to 7 minutes, or until the onion begins to brown. Add the garlic and cook for 1 minute. Stir in the thyme, parsley, ½ teaspoon of the salt and ¼ teaspoon of the pepper. Remove from the pot and set aside.

Season the pork with the remaining teaspoon of salt and ½ teaspoon of pepper. Add the oil to the pot, then the pork, and cook for 2 to 3 minutes, until browned on all sides. Add the apple juice and cook for 1 minute to deglaze, then add the apple. Turn the pot to HIGH pressure, secure the lid, adjust the valve to sealing and set the timer for 20 minutes. When the time is up, do a quick release by turning the valve to venting. Once finished, release the lid.

Remove the pork from the pot. Return the bacon mixture and stir in the cornstarch mixture until thickened. Slice the pork and serve with the sauce on top.

Pulled Pork with Texas Toast

Originally, this recipe was for baby back ribs, but for cost-effectiveness, I adjusted it instead to be a juicy and flavorful pulled pork. Beginning with my favorite rub mixture and tossed together with a homemade barbecue sauce, then served on garlic Texas toast, it's a simple yet flavorful meal!

Serves 6

$2.62 per serving

½ cup (100 g) light brown sugar

1 tbsp (7 g) paprika

1 tsp freshly ground black pepper

1 tsp salt

1 tsp chili powder

2 tsp (6 g) garlic powder

2 tsp (5 g) onion powder

½ tsp cayenne pepper

2½ lb (1.1 kg) boneless pork shoulder

1 cup (240 ml) water

1 (11.25-oz [319-g]) package garlic Texas toast

Barbecue Sauce

1 cup (240 g) ketchup

2 tbsp (30 ml) cider vinegar

⅓ cup (75 g) light brown sugar

1 tbsp (15 ml) Worcestershire sauce

¼ tsp liquid smoke

1 tsp paprika

½ tsp chili powder

¼ tsp salt

¼ tsp freshly ground black pepper

¼ tsp garlic powder

In a small bowl, combine the brown sugar, paprika, black pepper, salt, chili powder, garlic powder, onion powder and cayenne. Rub the mixture over the pork, ensuring it's covered on all sides.

Place the trivet in the pot, place the pork inside and add the water. Turn the pot to HIGH pressure, secure the lid, adjust the valve to sealing and set the timer for 50 minutes. When the time is up, do a quick release by turning the valve to venting. Once finished, release the lid.

Meanwhile, prepare the barbecue sauce: In a small pan over medium heat, stir together the ketchup, vinegar, brown sugar, Worcestershire, liquid smoke, paprika, chili powder, salt, black pepper and garlic powder. Bring the sauce to a simmer. Remove from the heat. Cook the toast according to the package directions.

Remove the pork from the pot and, using two forks, carefully shred the pork. Transfer the shredded pork to a large bowl and stir in the barbecue sauce. Serve over slices of Texas toast.

Lemon-Dill Chicken

Simple ingredients make some of the best—and most affordable—meals, and this recipe is no exception! Lemon and dill are one of those flavor pairings that everyone loves; adding it to chicken really makes this a standout dish. Don't forget that sauce in the pot: Pour it on top so you don't miss an ounce of flavor!

Serves 6

$1.65 per serving

1½ lbs (680 g) boneless, skinless chicken thighs

1 tsp salt

½ tsp freshly ground black pepper

1 tbsp (15 ml) canola oil

1 tbsp (14 g) unsalted butter

1 small onion, diced

3 cloves garlic, minced

1 cup (240 ml) chicken broth

2 tsp (2 g) dried dill, divided

2 tbsp (30 ml) fresh lemon juice

1½ cups (293 g) uncooked basmati rice, for serving (optional)

2 tsp (5 g) cornstarch mixed with 2 tsp (10 ml) water

Season the chicken with the salt and pepper. Turn the pot to sauté mode on HIGH until the screen says hot. Add the oil and butter and heat until melted, then the chicken, and cook for 2 to 4 minutes per side, or until browned. Remove from the pot and set aside. Add the onion and garlic to the pot, and cook for 5 to 7 minutes, or until the onion is translucent.

Stir in the broth, 1 teaspoon of the dill and the lemon juice. Return the chicken to the pot. Turn the pot to HIGH pressure, secure the lid, adjust the valve to sealing and set the timer for 10 minutes. When the time is up, do a quick release by turning the valve to venting. Once finished, release the lid.

Meanwhile, if serving with rice, cook according to the package directions.

Remove the chicken from the pot. Stir the cornstarch mixture into the pot until thickened. Serve the chicken topped with the sauce and the remaining teaspoon of dill. Serve alongside the rice (if using).

Spinach and Artichoke Chicken

This appetizer-inspired dinner smothers chicken with creamy spinach and artichoke sauce. Served over noodles, it's a hearty meal the whole family will love. Have leftover sauce? It's a great dip for garlic bread!

Serves 6

$2.04 per serving

1½ lbs (680 g) boneless, skinless chicken thighs

1 tsp salt

½ tsp freshly ground black pepper

1 tbsp (15 ml) canola oil

1 clove garlic, minced

1 (14-oz [397-g]) can quartered artichoke hearts, drained and chopped

1 cup (240 ml) chicken broth

1 (1-lb [455-g]) package egg noodles

4 cups (120 g) fresh baby spinach

1 (16-oz [473-ml]) jar Alfredo sauce

1 cup (115 g) shredded mozzarella cheese

2 tbsp (16 g) cornstarch mixed with 2 tbsp (30 ml) water

Season the chicken with the salt and pepper. Turn the pot to sauté mode on HIGH until the screen says hot. Add the oil, then the chicken, and cook for 2 to 4 minutes per side, or until browned. Remove from the pot and set aside. Add the garlic to the pot and cook for 30 seconds. Stir in the artichokes and broth, and cook for 1 minute to deglaze the pot, and return the chicken to the pot. Turn the pot to HIGH pressure, secure the lid, adjust the valve to sealing and set the timer for 8 minutes. When the time is up, do a quick release by turning the valve to venting. Once finished, release the lid.

Meanwhile, cook the egg noodles according to the package directions.

Turn the pot to sauté mode on HIGH. Remove the chicken from the pot and set aside. Add the spinach to the pot and stir for 5 minutes, until fully wilted. Stir in the Alfredo sauce and mozzarella until fully melted and combined. Stir in the cornstarch mixture until thickened. Serve the chicken and sauce over the noodles.

Beer-Braised Beef Cottage Pie

As its name suggests, this cottage pie has a beer-based gravy that pairs perfectly with the budget-friendly cut of tender beef and mashed potato topping. Best of all, everything is cooked at the same time and is quickly finished off in the oven. A time-saving trick for a comfort food staple that won't break the bank.

Serves 8

$2.59 per serving

2½ lb (1.1 kg) chuck roast, fat trimmed off, cut into ½" (1.3-cm) pieces

1 tsp salt, plus more to taste

½ tsp freshly ground black pepper, plus more to taste

2 tbsp (30 ml) canola oil, divided

1 large onion, diced

1 large carrot, sliced

1 celery rib, sliced

3 cloves garlic, minced

1 (12-oz [355-ml]) bottle beer

1 (14.5-oz [429-ml]) can beef broth

2 thyme sprigs

1½ lbs (680 g) russet potatoes, peeled and quartered

¼ cup (32 g) cornstarch, mixed with ¼ cup (60 ml) water

¼ cup (55 g/½ stick) unsalted butter

½ cup (120 ml) milk

Note: If you do not have the handled steamer pan and the tall egg rack, you can make the potatoes on the stovetop by boiling them in salted water for 20 minutes, until fork-tender.

Season the beef with the salt and pepper. Turn the pot to sauté mode on HIGH until the screen says hot. Add 1 tablespoon (15 ml) of the oil and, working in batches, add the beef, and cook for 2 to 3 minutes per side, or until browned. Remove from the pot and set aside. Add the remaining tablespoon (15 ml) of oil to the pot, then the onion, and cook for 10 to 12 minutes, until starting to brown. Add the carrot, celery and garlic, and cook, stirring occasionally, for 2 to 4 minutes, or until just softened. Add the beer to the pot, and cook, stirring occasionally, for 7 to 10 minutes, or until reduced by more than half. Add the broth and thyme, and return the beef to the pot.

Place the tall egg rack in the pot just above the meat mixture. Place the handled steamer pan on top and place the potatoes inside. Turn the pot to HIGH pressure, secure the lid, adjust the valve to sealing and set the timer for 40 minutes. When the time is up, do a quick release by turning the valve to venting. Once finished, release the lid.

Remove the pan and rack from the pot. Remove the thyme sprigs and stir in the cornstarch mixture until thickened. Pour the beef mixture into a 12-inch (30-cm) baking dish.

Set the oven to broil on HIGH. In a large bowl, mash together the potatoes and butter. Gradually add the milk and season with salt and pepper to taste. Gently spoon the mashed potatoes over the beef mixture. Place in the oven for about 5 minutes and broil, watching carefully, until the potatoes are golden and crisp.

Cajun Chicken Jambalaya

This Cajun stew packs a little bit of a kick and a whole lot of flavor! In just a few short steps you have a Cajun dinner on the table in no time. The chicken thighs and rice make this a frugal meal that will wow your taste buds.

Serves 6

$2.72 per serving

2 tbsp (30 ml) canola oil, divided

12 oz (340 g) andouille sausage, cut into ¼" (6-mm) slices

1 lb (455 g) boneless, skinless chicken thighs, cut into ½" (1.3-cm) pieces

1 medium-sized onion, diced

1 green bell pepper, seeded and diced

1 celery rib, diced

3 cloves garlic, minced

1 (10-oz [280-g]) can diced tomatoes with green chiles

2 tsp (5 g) Cajun seasoning, or more as desired

½ tsp salt

1 (14.5-oz [429-ml]) can chicken broth

1 cup (195 g) uncooked basmati rice

4 green onions, thinly sliced, for serving

Turn the pot to sauté mode on HIGH until the screen says hot. Add 1 tablespoon (15 ml) of the oil, then the sausage, and cook for 2 to 4 minutes per side, or until browned. Remove from the pot and set aside. Add the remaining tablespoon (15 ml) of oil to the pot, add the chicken, and cook for 2 to 4 minutes, or until browned on all sides. Remove and set aside.

Add the onion, bell pepper, celery and garlic to the pot, and cook for 5 to 7 minutes, or until softened. Stir in the tomatoes, Cajun seasoning, salt and broth. Return the chicken to the pot. Pour the rice over the top. Turn the pot to HIGH pressure, secure the lid, adjust the valve to sealing and set the timer for 15 minutes. When the time is up, do a quick release by turning the valve to venting. Once finished, release the lid.

Return the sausage to the pot and stir until heated through. Serve topped with the green onions.

Inside-Out Stuffed Cabbage

Stuffed cabbage is delicious but can be a bit tedious to put together. I took this already budget-friendly meal and turned it into one that is much quicker to make. The results are a quick-to-cook stuffed cabbage stew fit for any night of the week!

Serves 6

$2.31 per serving

1 lb (455 g) ground beef

1 tsp salt

¼ tsp freshly ground black pepper

1 small onion, diced

2 cloves garlic, minced

¼ cup (60 g) ketchup

1 tbsp (2 g) dried basil

1 (32-oz [946-ml]) container beef broth

1 cup (240 ml) water

1 (14.5-oz [429-ml]) can tomato sauce

¼ cup (50 g) light brown sugar

¼ cup (60 ml) fresh lemon juice

¼ cup (60 ml) Worcestershire sauce

1 medium-sized cabbage, cut into 2" (5-cm) pieces

1 cup (195 g) uncooked basmati rice

Turn the pot to sauté mode on HIGH until the screen says hot. Add the beef, salt and pepper, and cook for 5 to 7 minutes, or until no longer pink. Add the onion and cook for 4 to 5 minutes, or until just softened. Add the garlic and cook for 1 minute.

Stir in the ketchup, basil, broth, water, tomato sauce, brown sugar, lemon juice, Worcestershire and cabbage. Pour the rice on top. Turn the pot to HIGH pressure, secure the lid, adjust the valve to sealing and set the timer for 10 minutes. When the time is up, do a quick release by turning the valve to venting. Once finished, release the lid.

Sicilian Beef Stew with Polenta

This is a beef stew unlike any I've tried before. Making your own homemade polenta is a money saver here, as buying premade is more expensive than most people realize. Cooked with fennel, orange and rosemary, this aromatic stew dives into a Sicilian flavor profile many have yet to discover. It looks and feels fancy but without the fancy price tag.

Serves 8

$2.90 per serving

2½ lb (1.1 kg) beef chuck, patted dry and cut into 2" (5-cm) pieces

1 tbsp (18 g) + 2 tsp (12 g) salt, divided

1 tsp freshly ground black pepper

¼ cup (60 ml) canola oil

2 medium-sized onions, sliced

1½ cups (355 ml) red wine

1 fennel bulb, cut into ½" (1.3-cm) wedges

4 cloves garlic, minced

1 large bay leaf

1 (3" [7.5-cm]) strip orange peel

2 rosemary sprigs

½ tsp dried thyme

3 tbsp (48 g) tomato paste

1 (14.5-oz [429-ml]) can beef broth

1 (28-oz [800-g]) can crushed tomatoes

1½ tsp (2 g) red pepper flakes (optional)

4 cups (946 ml) water

2 cups (475 ml) milk

1½ cups (210 g) yellow cornmeal

¼ cup (55 g/½ stick) unsalted butter

1 cup (100 g) whole pitted green Spanish olives

Season the beef with 2 teaspoons (12 g) of the salt and all of the black pepper. Turn the pot to sauté mode on HIGH until the screen says hot. Add the oil, then the beef, and cook for 4 minutes per side, or until browned. Remove from the pot and set aside. Add the onions to the pot and cook for 5 to 7 minutes, or until translucent. Add the wine and cook for 3 to 5 minutes, or until it has almost evaporated.

Stir in the fennel, garlic, bay leaf, orange peel, rosemary, thyme, tomato paste, broth, tomatoes and red pepper flakes (if using). Return the beef to the pot. Turn the pot to HIGH pressure, secure the lid, adjust the valve to sealing and set the timer for 40 minutes. When the time is up, do a quick release by turning the valve to venting. Once finished, release the lid.

Meanwhile, in a medium-sized pot over medium-high heat, combine the water, milk and remaining tablespoon (18 g) of salt. Once at a simmer, slowly stir in the cornmeal and cook for 2 to 3 minutes. Lower the heat to LOW and cook, stirring occasionally, for 40 minutes. Stir the butter into the polenta until fully melted.

Add the olives and remove the bay leaf, rosemary and orange peel. Serve the stew over the polenta.

Shredded BBQ Beef Sandwiches

Barbecue may just be a universal crowd-pleaser, and luckily for you, this recipe will feed that crowd too! Tender shredded beef gets slathered in a tangy homemade barbecue sauce that will save you money compared to store-bought. It's simple and delicious; what more could you ask for?

Serves 8

$2.01 per serving

3 lb (1.4 kg) beef chuck roast, fat trimmed off, cut into 2 pieces

2 tsp (12 g) salt

1 tsp freshly ground black pepper

2 tbsp (30 ml) canola oil, divided

1 medium-sized onion, sliced

1½ cups (355 ml) beef broth

1 to 2 cups (240 to 475 ml) barbecue sauce, or to taste

8 hamburger or brioche buns

Barbecue Sauce

1 cup (240 g) ketchup

2 tbsp (30 ml) cider vinegar

⅓ cup (75 g) light brown sugar

1 tbsp (15 ml) Worcestershire sauce

1 tsp paprika

¼ tsp liquid smoke

½ tsp chili powder

¼ tsp salt

¼ tsp freshly ground black pepper

¼ tsp garlic powder

⅛ tsp cayenne pepper (optional)

Season the beef with the salt and black pepper. Turn the pot to sauté mode on HIGH until the screen says hot.

Add 1 tablespoon (15 ml) of the oil, then the beef, working in batches if necessary, and cook for 3 to 4 minutes per side, or until browned. Remove from the pot and set aside. Add the remaining tablespoon (15 ml) of oil to the pot, then the onion, and cook for 12 to 15 minutes, or until browned and starting to caramelize.

Add the broth, then return the beef to the pot. Turn the pot to HIGH pressure, secure the lid, adjust the valve to sealing and set the timer for 50 minutes. When the time is up, do a quick release by turning the valve to venting. Once finished, release the lid.

Meanwhile, prepare the barbecue sauce: In a small pan over medium heat, combine the ketchup, vinegar, brown sugar, Worcestershire, paprika, liquid smoke, chili powder, salt, black pepper, garlic powder and cayenne (if using). Stirring constantly, bring the mixture to a simmer, then remove from the heat. Allow to cool.

Remove the beef from the pot and, using two forks, carefully shred the beef. Transfer the beef to a large bowl and stir in the barbecue sauce. Serve on toasted buns.

Steakhouse Sandwich

Just when you were sure you had made the most out of a roast, let me introduce you to another fun way to prepare it, all while saving money. Served in a toasted sandwich roll and topped with melty Swiss cheese and a homemade creamy onion sauce, this really makes a simple yet showstopping meal.

Serves 8

$2.52 per serving

3 lb (1.4 kg) beef chuck roast, cut into 3 pieces

2 tsp (12 g) salt

1 tsp freshly ground black pepper

3 tbsp (45 ml) canola oil, divided

1 large onion, sliced

3 cloves garlic, minced

1 (14.5-oz [429-ml]) can beef broth

1 tsp dried oregano

1 tsp onion powder

1 tsp paprika

½ tsp garlic powder

8 slices Swiss cheese

8 (6" [15-cm]) hoagie or sandwich rolls

Sauce

½ cup (120 ml) prepared Alfredo sauce

¼ cup (60 g) mayonnaise

½ tsp onion powder

½ tsp garlic powder

½ tsp salt

¼ tsp freshly ground black pepper

Season the beef with the salt and pepper. Turn the pot to sauté mode on HIGH until the screen says hot. Add 2 tablespoons (30 ml) of the oil, then the beef, working in batches if necessary, and cook for 3 to 4 minutes per side, or until browned. Remove and set aside. Add the remaining tablespoon (15 ml) of oil, then the onion, and cook for 12 to 15 minutes, or until browned and starting to caramelize. Remove ¼ cup (40 g) of the onion from the pot and set aside.

Add the garlic to the pot and cook for 1 minute. Stir in the broth, oregano, onion powder, paprika and garlic powder, then return the beef to the pot. Turn the pot to HIGH pressure, secure the lid, adjust the valve to sealing and set the timer for 50 minutes. When the time is up, do a quick release by turning the valve to venting. Once finished, release the lid.

Meanwhile, prepare the sauce: Mince the reserved cooked onion into a paste. In a small bowl, stir together the Alfredo sauce, mayo, onion powder, garlic powder, salt, pepper and minced onion. Cover and refrigerate until ready to serve.

Set the oven to broil on HIGH. Remove the beef from the pot and, using two forks, carefully shred the beef and return it to its liquid. Add the cheese to the hoagies and broil for about 2 minutes, until toasted and melted. Spread the sauce on the bun, add the shredded beef and serve with a side of the pan juices for dipping.

Oregano Chicken Pitas with Tzatziki

This savory sandwich comes together with little fuss and is loaded in a pita with a fresh vegetable salad and a tangy tzatziki sauce. Making your own sauce at home is both more flavorful and cheaper than you can buy in stores. This is my take on the Greek-inspired comfort food!

Serves 6

$2.83 per serving

Yogurt Sauce

1 cup (230 g) Greek yogurt
1 tbsp (15 ml) fresh lemon juice
1 tbsp (15 ml) extra virgin olive oil
1 tbsp (4 g) chopped fresh dill
½ tsp salt
½ tsp garlic powder
Freshly ground black pepper

2 lbs (905 g) boneless, skinless chicken thighs
1 tsp salt
½ tsp freshly ground pepper
2 tbsp (30 ml) canola oil
2 tbsp (28 g) unsalted butter, melted
¼ cup (60 ml) fresh lemon juice
2 tbsp (30 ml) Worcestershire sauce
2 tbsp (30 ml) low-sodium soy sauce
2 tsp (2 g) dried oregano
1 tsp garlic powder
6 Greek-style pita flatbreads

Salad

2 small tomatoes, diced
2 shallots, sliced
1 small cucumber, diced
1 tsp extra virgin olive oil
½ tsp salt
Freshly ground black pepper

In a medium-sized bowl, prepare the yogurt sauce: Stir together the yogurt, lemon juice, oil, dill, salt, garlic powder and pepper to taste. Cover and refrigerate until ready to serve.

Season the chicken with the salt and pepper. In a small bowl, stir together the oil, butter, lemon juice, Worcestershire, soy sauce, oregano and garlic powder. Combine the sauce and chicken in the pot. Turn the pot to HIGH pressure, secure the lid, adjust the valve to sealing and set the timer for 10 minutes. When the time is up, do a quick release by turning the valve to venting. Once finished, release the lid.

Meanwhile, in a medium-sized bowl, prepare the salad: Toss together the tomatoes, shallots, cucumber, oil, salt and pepper to taste.

Remove the chicken from the pot, let sit for 5 minutes and then slice. Return the chicken to the pot until ready to serve. Serve in warm pitas with the salad then the sauce on top.

Pasta-bilities

Whether it be short, long, thin or wide, pasta comes in just about every shape and size imaginable. When it comes to convenience, I'm not sure what could stand up against it. It can go from the pantry to the dinner table in around fifteen minutes or less. What's not to love about that? Although it is already a great option for the budget, grocers commonly have pasta on sale, making it perfect to stock up on, and it fills you up. It can be served with just about anything, and that speaks to just how versatile it really is. This chapter gives just a glimpse of what you can do with pasta in your Instant Pot, and I hope it inspires you to come up with your own recipes, too!

Kicking Cajun Pasta

Pasta with a little kick! When a busy day gets the better of you and dinner needs to be something quick and flavorful, this pasta is it. With some being hotter than others, no two Cajun seasonings are really alike. If you're concerned about spice, don't be afraid to hold back and season as you go.

Serves 6

$2.30 per serving

2 lbs (905 g) boneless, skinless chicken thighs, cut into 1" (2.5-cm) pieces

1 tsp salt

½ tsp freshly ground black pepper

2 tbsp (30 ml) canola oil

1 (32-oz [946-ml]) container chicken broth

1 (14.5-oz [411-g]) can Mexican stewed tomatoes

2 cloves garlic, minced

1 (1-lb [455-g]) package penne pasta

1 tbsp (7 g) Cajun seasoning, or to heat preference

2 cups (475 ml) half-and-half

1 cup (115 g) shredded Cheddar cheese

1 tbsp (8 g) cornstarch mixed with 1 tbsp (15 ml) water

2 green onions, sliced, for serving

Season the chicken with the salt and pepper. Turn the pot to sauté mode on HIGH until the screen says hot. Add the oil, then the chicken, and cook for 2 to 3 minutes per side, or until browned on all sides. Remove from the pot and set aside.

Add the broth to the pot and stir to deglaze. Stir in the tomatoes, garlic, pasta and Cajun seasoning, then return the chicken to the pot and stir. Turn the pot to HIGH pressure, secure the lid, adjust the valve to sealing and set the timer for 8 minutes. When the time is up, do a quick release by turning the valve to venting. Once finished, release the lid.

Turn the pot to sauté mode on HIGH. Stir in the half-and-half and cheese until melted. Stir in the cornstarch mixture until thickened. Serve topped with the green onions.

Italian Sausage Bolognese

A meat sauce that doesn't have to simmer for hours to develop its flavor is a winner for anyone. This traditional meat sauce uses cost-effective Italian sausage as the base for its incredible flavor; also, the seasonings in the sausage reduce the amount of ingredients needed for this recipe, keeping the ingredient list simple. Cooking under pressure develops the flavors that you usually only get from cooking for hours on the stovetop. Simply serve this sauce over your favorite pasta or layer with it to create an incredible lasagna.

Serves 8

$2.16 per serving

2 tbsp (30 ml) canola oil

1 medium-sized onion, diced

2 celery ribs, diced

1 carrot, diced

2 cloves garlic, minced

2 lbs (905 g) ground Italian sausage

½ cup (120 ml) red wine

1 cup (240 ml) whole milk

1 (14.5-oz [411-g]) can diced tomatoes

2 (28-oz [828-ml]) cans tomato sauce

1 tsp salt

1 tbsp (1 g) dried parsley

1 tbsp (3 g) dried oregano

½ tsp freshly ground black pepper

1 tsp onion powder

1 tsp garlic powder

1 (1-lb [455-g]) package spaghetti pasta

Turn the pot to sauté mode on HIGH until the screen says hot. Add the oil, then the onion, celery and carrot, and cook for 5 to 7 minutes, or until softened. Add the garlic and sausage, and cook for 12 to 15 minutes, or until no longer pink.

Stir in the wine and milk; bring to a rapid simmer, and simmer for 15 minutes, or until reduced by half. Stir in the tomatoes, tomato sauce, salt, parsley, oregano, pepper, onion powder and garlic powder. Turn the pot to HIGH pressure, secure the lid, adjust the valve to sealing and set the timer for 15 minutes. When the time is up, do a quick release by turning the valve to venting. Once finished, release the lid.

Remove the lid from the pot and let rest for 15 minutes before serving. Meanwhile, cook the pasta according to the package directions. Serve the sauce over the pasta.

Caramelized Onion and Mushroom Pasta

Sometimes simple ingredients make some of the most outstanding meals, and this pasta is no exception! With a little care and time, the onions become caramelized and create the base flavor of the whole dish, keeping the ingredients and the cost low. Add some cream and baby spinach to make this a complete meal.

Serves 4

$2.53 per serving

¼ cup (60 ml) canola oil

2 large onions, thinly sliced

1 tsp salt

8 oz (225 g) button mushrooms, quartered

1 (14.5-oz [429-ml]) can chicken broth

8 oz (225 g) fettuccine pasta, broken in half

1 cup (240 ml) half-and-half

1 cup (100 g) grated Parmesan cheese

3 cups (90 g) baby spinach

Turn the pot to sauté mode on HIGH until the screen says hot. Add the oil, then the onions and salt, and cook for 30 minutes, or until the onions start to caramelize to a dark golden brown. Add the mushrooms and cook for 10 minutes, or until they start to brown and soften. Stir in the broth and pasta until the pasta is submerged. Turn the pot to HIGH pressure, secure the lid, adjust the valve to sealing and set the timer for 7 minutes. When the time is up, do a quick release by turning the valve to venting. Once finished, release the lid.

Turn the pot to sauté mode on HIGH. Cook for 10 minutes, stirring continuously, to reduce the liquid by half. Stir in the half-and-half, Parmesan and spinach until the spinach is wilted and the cheese is melted.

Extra-Creamy Mac and Cheese

Mac and cheese needs no introduction since it is a staple in homes all over the world, but you'd be hard-pressed to find any that are exactly alike. Our one-pot mac and cheese keeps it simple and creamy, but don't be afraid to change it up. Swap the cheeses, add bacon or throw in some vegetables for a rich and nutritious meal!

Serves 4

$1.74 per serving

1 (1-lb [455-g]) package elbow pasta
2 cups (475 ml) water
1 (14.5-oz [429-ml]) can chicken broth
2 tsp (8 g) Dijon mustard
2 tsp (12 g) salt
½ tsp freshly ground black pepper
¼ cup (55 g/½ stick) unsalted butter
2 cups (475 ml) whole milk
8 oz (225 g) shredded sharp Cheddar cheese
8 oz (225 g) shredded Colby Jack cheese

Combine the noodles, water, broth, Dijon, salt and pepper in the pot. Turn the pot to HIGH pressure, secure the lid, adjust the valve to sealing and set the timer for 7 minutes. When the time is up, do a quick release by turning the valve to venting. Once finished, release the lid.

Turn the pot to sauté mode on LOW. Stir in the butter until melted. Add the milk, Cheddar and Colby Jack, stirring until completely melted and creamy.

Tortellini Alfredo with Italian Sausage

A simple crowd-pleaser that won't break the bank. Both rich and flavorful, this tortellini will make you feel like you're at the finest Italian restaurant—but right at home and without the hefty bill at the end! The Italian sausage keeps costs low and rounds this dish out to be a meal you will be coming back to again and again.

Serves 6

$2.16 per serving

1 tbsp (15 ml) canola oil

1 small onion, diced

4 cloves garlic, minced

1 lb (455 g) ground Italian sausage

1 (14.5-oz [429-ml]) can chicken broth

1 (20-oz [567-g]) package frozen cheese tortellini

1 tsp salt

½ tsp freshly ground black pepper

¾ cup (175 ml) heavy cream

4 oz (115 g) cream cheese, diced, softened

1 cup (100 g) grated Parmesan cheese

3 cups (90 g) baby spinach

Turn the pot to sauté mode on HIGH until the screen says hot. Add the oil, then the onion and garlic, and cook for 4 to 5 minutes, or until just softened. Add the sausage and cook for 12 to 15 minutes, or until no longer pink.

Stir in the broth, tortellini, salt and pepper. Turn the pot to HIGH pressure, secure the lid, adjust the valve to sealing and set the timer for 6 minutes. When the time is up, do a quick release by turning the valve to venting. Once finished, release the lid.

Turn the pot to sauté mode on HIGH. Stir in the cream, cream cheese, Parmesan and spinach, until the spinach is wilted.

Meatball Stroganoff with Egg Noodles

Beef Stroganoff is world famous and incredibly delicious. Instead of using strips of beef or steak, this budget-friendly take uses homemade meatballs, which makes this version slightly reminiscent of Swedish meatballs. The best part is everything cooks in the pot, leaving only one step before serving!

Serves 6

$2.99 per serving

½ cup (60 g) plain dried breadcrumbs

½ cup (120 ml) whole milk

1 tsp salt

½ tsp freshly ground black pepper

3 tbsp (45 ml) canola oil, divided

1 medium-sized onion, diced

1 lb (455 g) ground beef

1 lb (455 g) button mushrooms, halved

3 cups (710 ml) beef broth

1 tbsp (11 g) Dijon mustard

2 tbsp (30 ml) Worcestershire sauce

8 oz (225 g) egg noodles

⅓ cup (20 g) chopped fresh dill, divided

⅓ cup (77 g) sour cream

In a large bowl, combine the breadcrumbs, milk, salt and pepper.

Turn the pot to sauté mode on HIGH until the screen says hot. Add 1 tablespoon (15 ml) of the oil, then the onion, and cook for 10 to 12 minutes, or until lightly browned. Remove the onion from the pot and turn off the heat. Add ¼ cup (40 g) of the onion and the beef to the breadcrumb mixture. Using your hands, mix until fully combined, then form into 1-inch (2.5-cm) balls. Return the pot to sauté mode on HIGH. Add 1 tablespoon (15 ml) of the oil, then, working in batches, carefully place the meatballs in the pot and cook for 3 minutes per side, or until browned. Remove from the pot and set aside. Add the remaining tablespoon (15 ml) of oil, return the remaining onion to the pot, add the mushrooms and cook for 10 minutes, or until the mushrooms have softened.

Stir in the broth, Dijon, Worcestershire and noodles. Return the meatballs to the pot. Turn the pot to HIGH pressure, secure the lid, adjust the valve to sealing and set the timer for 5 minutes. When the time is up, do a quick release by turning the valve to venting. Once finished, release the lid.

Stir in ¼ cup (15 g) of the dill and the sour cream until fully combined. Serve topped with the remaining dill.

Macaroni and Beef

Mac and beef is a favorite in the frozen food aisle, so I made this into a recipe that is incredibly simple and an even more budget-friendly meal to make than buying it premade. It makes great leftovers, and it freezes so well you won't have to worry about wasting any!

Serves 8

$2.67 per serving

1 tbsp (15 ml) canola oil
1 large onion, diced
2 lbs (905 g) ground beef
2 tsp (12 g) seasoned salt
½ tsp freshly ground black pepper
1 green bell pepper, seeded and chopped
3 cloves garlic, minced
2 (15-oz [444-ml]) cans tomato sauce
2 (15-oz [425-g]) cans diced tomatoes
3 cups (710 ml) water
2 cups (210 g) elbow macaroni
3 tbsp (45 ml) Worcestershire sauce
2 tbsp (11 g) Italian seasoning
2 tsp (5 g) paprika
1 cup (115 g) shredded Cheddar cheese, for serving

Turn the pot to sauté mode on HIGH until the screen says hot. Add the oil, then the onion, and cook for 5 to 7 minutes, or until softened. Add the beef, seasoned salt and black pepper, and cook for 7 to 10 minutes, or until no longer pink. Add the bell pepper and garlic, and cook for 4 to 5 minutes, or until softened.

Stir in the tomato sauce, tomatoes, water, macaroni, Worcestershire, Italian seasoning and paprika. Turn the pot to HIGH pressure, secure the lid, adjust the valve to sealing and set the timer for 15 minutes. When the time is up, do a quick release by turning the valve to venting. Once finished, release the lid.

Serve in bowls topped with the shredded cheese.

Shredded Pork Ragu

Most commonly served with pasta, ragu is an Italian meat sauce that's quite versatile. It can also be seen served in a sandwich—like an Italian sloppy joe of sorts. The budget-friendly pork roast is simmered in a rich tomato sauce, resulting in tender, fall-off-the-bone meat.

Serves 8

$2.45 per serving

2 tbsp (30 ml) canola oil, divided
3 lb (1.4 kg) pork roast, cut into 2 pieces
2 tsp (12 g) salt
1 tsp freshly ground black pepper
1 medium-sized onion, finely diced
1 carrot, shredded
1 celery rib, finely diced
3 cloves garlic, minced
1 tbsp (3 g) dried oregano
1½ tsp (3 g) dried thyme
½ cup (120 ml) red wine
1 (28-oz [800-g]) can crushed tomatoes
1 (6-oz [170-g]) can tomato paste
1 (1-lb [455-g]) package egg noodles
Grated Parmesan, for serving (optional)

Turn the pot to sauté mode on HIGH until the screen says hot. Add 1 tablespoon (15 ml) of the oil. Season the pork with the salt and pepper on all sides. Add the pork to the pot, one piece at a time. Brown for about 3 to 5 minutes per side, on all sides, then repeat with the second piece. Remove from the pot and set aside.

Add the remaining tablespoon (15 ml) of oil to the pot. Add the onion, carrot, celery, garlic, oregano and thyme, and cook for 5 to 7 minutes, or until the onion is translucent. Add the red wine and cook 5 to 7 minutes, or until reduced by half. Stir in the tomatoes and tomato paste. Add the pork back to the pot. Turn the pot to HIGH pressure, secure the lid, adjust the valve to sealing and set the timer for 40 minutes. When the time is up, do a quick release by turning the valve to venting. Once finished, release the lid.

Meanwhile, in a large pot, bring water to a boil and cook the pasta according to the package directions. Reserve ½ cup (120 ml) of pasta water before draining.

Remove the pork from the pot and, using two forks, carefully shred the pork and return it to the pot. Stir the pasta and reserved water into the pot. Serve topped with Parmesan (if using).

Wokless Cooking

Cooking Asian-style meals in an Instant Pot may seem like a far stretch, but I promise these recipes come together so well, you won't want to make them any other way! From fun modifications on classics such as eggrolls (page 89) and lettuce cups (page 78) to a flavorful pho (page 90) and red coconut curry (page 93), this chapter is filled with great recipes that you'll be making again and again. Using budget-friendly cuts of meat and reducing the list of ingredients to only the necessary items—none of those hard-to-find ingredients that don't add much to the recipe—make these meals great on the wallet and still high on flavor.

Sticky Honey Garlic Chicken

These budget-friendly chicken thighs are so good, they're borderline addictive! They have a perfect salty-sweet glaze that makes it incredibly hard to resist. Not to mention this dish comes together so easily, you'll be making it again and again!

Serves 6

$2.38 per serving

1½ lbs (680 g) boneless, skinless chicken thighs

1 tsp salt

½ tsp freshly ground black pepper

3 tbsp (60 g) honey

1 tsp light brown sugar

4 cloves garlic, minced

2 tbsp (30 ml) soy sauce

½ cup (120 ml) chicken broth

1 tbsp (15 ml) Sriracha

1 tbsp (15 ml) canola oil

3 cups (510 g) cooked rice, for serving (optional)

1 green onion, thinly sliced, for serving

Season the chicken with the salt and pepper. In a small bowl, combine the honey, brown sugar, garlic, soy sauce, broth and Sriracha, then set aside.

Turn the pot to sauté mode on HIGH until the screen says hot. Add the oil, then the chicken, and cook for 3 to 4 minutes, or until browned on both sides. Pour in the sauce. Turn the pot to HIGH pressure, secure the lid, adjust the valve to sealing and set the timer for 10 minutes. When the time is up, do a quick release by turning the valve to venting. Once finished, release the lid.

Meanwhile, if serving with rice, cook according to the package directions.

Remove the chicken and set aside. Turn the pot to sauté mode on HIGH and cook for 5 minutes, or until the sauce has reduced to about ½ cup (120 ml) of glaze. Pour the glaze over the chicken, serve with a side of rice (if using) and garnish with the green onion.

Easy Chicken Lettuce Wraps

One of my favorite appetizers has to be lettuce wraps. From the texture to the fun way to eat them, and the savory sauce, I'm not sure which is my favorite part. The only way to really improve on them was to make a bigger batch so they can be a dinner. They are cheaper and better than going to a Chinese restaurant.

Serves 6

$2.99 per serving

1 tbsp (15 ml) canola oil

1 lb (455 g) ground chicken

1 tsp salt

½ tsp freshly ground black pepper

1 medium-sized onion, diced

1 carrot, diced

1 celery rib, sliced

3 cloves garlic, minced

½ cup (120 ml) chicken broth

¼ cup (60 ml) hoisin sauce

¼ cup (60 ml) soy sauce

1 tbsp (15 ml) rice vinegar

2 tbsp (30 ml) sweet chili sauce

1 tbsp (6 g) grated fresh ginger

1 tsp Sriracha (optional)

2 tbsp (25 g) light brown sugar

1 (8-oz [225-g]) can sliced water chestnuts, drained

1 tbsp (8 g) cornstarch mixed with 1 tbsp (15 ml) water

1 head iceberg lettuce, cut in half and leaves separated

2 green onions, thinly sliced, for garnish

Turn the pot to sauté mode on HIGH until the screen says hot. Add the oil, then the chicken, salt and pepper, and cook for 4 to 5 minutes, or until opaque. Add the onion, carrot and celery, and cook for 5 to 7 minutes, or until the onion is softened. Add the garlic and cook for 2 minutes.

Stir in the chicken broth, hoisin sauce, soy sauce, rice vinegar, chili sauce, ginger, Sriracha (if using), brown sugar and water chestnuts. Turn the pot to HIGH pressure, secure the lid, adjust the valve to sealing and set the timer for 6 minutes. When the time is up, do a quick release by turning the valve to venting. Once finished, release the lid.

Turn the pot to sauté mode on LOW and simmer for 10 minutes, or until the liquid reduces by half. Stir in the cornstarch mixture until thickened. Serve in lettuce leaves and top with the green onions.

Mongolian Beef and Mushrooms

Here, tender chunks of flank steak are bathed in a homemade savory sauce. Cooked with mushrooms and topped off with fresh green onions, serving this over rice makes this cost-effective, simple meal feel extra special with a taste you won't forget.

Serves 6

$2.90 per serving

1½ lb (680 g) flank steak, sliced into ½" (1.3-cm) pieces

¼ cup (32 g) cornstarch

1 tsp sesame oil

4 cloves garlic, minced

½ cup (100 g) light brown sugar

½ cup (120 ml) low-sodium soy sauce

½ tsp ground ginger

1 cup (240 ml) water

1 tbsp (15 ml) rice vinegar

1 tsp Sriracha

¼ cup (60 ml) canola oil

8 oz (225 g) button mushrooms, quartered

1½ cups (293 g) uncooked basmati rice, for serving (optional)

3 green onions, sliced

In a resealable plastic bag, toss the steak with the cornstarch to coat. In a small bowl, combine the sesame oil, garlic, brown sugar, soy sauce, ginger, water, rice vinegar and Sriracha, then set this sauce mixture aside. Turn the pot to sauté mode on HIGH until the screen says hot. Add the canola oil. Working in batches, add the steak and cook for 3 to 4 minutes, per side, or until just browned.

Stir the sauce mixture and mushrooms into the pot. Turn the pot to HIGH pressure, secure the lid, adjust the valve to sealing and set the timer for 25 minutes. When the time is up, do a quick release by turning the valve to venting. Once finished, release the lid.

Meanwhile, if serving with rice, cook according to the package directions.

Stir the mixture and serve with rice (if using), topped with the green onions.

Sweet Soy Pork Roast

A few simple steps are all it takes for a delicious and inexpensive pork dinner. With meat so deliciously tender and a sauce that tantalizes every taste bud, this meal is one that makes you want seconds.

Serves 6

$2.12 per serving

2½ lb (1.1 kg) boneless pork loin or roast

½ cup (120 ml) soy sauce

½ cup (120 ml) water

¼ cup (50 g) light brown sugar

1 tsp ground ginger

2 cloves garlic, minced

1 tbsp (15 ml) toasted sesame oil

1 tbsp (15 ml) Sriracha

1½ cups (293 g) uncooked basmati rice, for serving (optional)

2 tbsp (16 g) cornstarch mixed with 2 tbsp (30 ml) water

Place the pork in the pot. In a small bowl, stir together the soy sauce, water, brown sugar, ginger, garlic, sesame oil and Sriracha until the sugar dissolves. Pour the sauce mixture into the pot.

Turn the pot to HIGH pressure, secure the lid, adjust the valve to sealing and set the timer for 30 minutes. When the time is up, do a quick release by turning the valve to venting. Once finished, release the lid.

Meanwhile, if serving with rice, cook according to the package directions.

Remove the pork from the pot and stir in the cornstarch mixture. Slice the pork and serve with the sauce over the top and with a side of rice (if using).

BBQ Korean Beef

While slightly more complicated than some of the other recipes featured in this chapter, this recipe is worth every minute. Marinated in a delicious sauce that adds extra flavor without any extra ingredients, this beef is tasty through and through, only made better by reducing that sauce into a sticky glaze. Serve it over rice, and it's a dinner fit for a crowd.

Serves 8

$2.98 per serving

1 large onion, half chopped, half sliced, divided

½ cup (120 ml) beef broth

⅓ cup (80 ml) low-sodium soy sauce

⅓ cup (75 g) light brown sugar

4 cloves garlic, minced

2 tbsp (30 ml) sesame oil

1 tbsp (15 ml) rice vinegar

1 tsp ground ginger

1 tsp Sriracha, or more to taste

3 lb (1.4 kg) boneless beef chuck roast, cut into 1" (2.5-cm) pieces

1½ cups (293 g) uncooked basmati rice, for serving (optional)

2 green onions, thinly sliced, for serving

In a blender, combine the chopped onion, beef broth, soy sauce, brown sugar, garlic, sesame oil, rice vinegar, ginger and Sriracha. Blend the mixture until smooth. Place the beef in a large bowl and pour the mixture over the beef. Let sit for 20 minutes in the refrigerator.

Add the beef and sauce to the pot. Turn the pot to HIGH pressure, secure the lid, adjust the valve to sealing and set the timer for 20 minutes. When the time is up, do a quick release by turning the valve to venting. Once finished, release the lid.

Meanwhile, if serving with rice, cook according to the package directions.

Turn the pot to sauté mode on HIGH. Stir in the sliced onion and cook for 25 minutes, or until the sauce is reduced and thickened, stirring occasionally. Serve over rice (if using), topped with the green onions.

Pork with Pineapple, Red Onion and Peppers

Savory with a bit of sweet, this pork packs in the flavor. It is paired with pineapple, peppers and red onion and served with a simple sauce. Inexpensive ingredients come together to make this showstopping and incredibly satisfying meal.

Serves 6

$2.94 **per serving**

Sauce

2 tbsp (30 ml) canola oil

½ cup (120 ml) condensed orange juice

¼ cup (60 ml) teriyaki sauce

2 tbsp (40 g) honey

¼ tsp red pepper flakes (optional)

¼ cup (50 g) light brown sugar

1 cup (240 ml) chicken broth

¼ cup (32 g) cornstarch mixed with ¼ cup (60 ml) water

2 lb (905 g) pork tenderloin

2 cups (330 g) fresh pineapple chunks

1 red bell pepper, seeded and cut into ¼" (6-mm) slices

1 orange bell pepper, seeded and cut into ¼" (6-mm) slices

1 medium-sized red onion, cut into ¼" (6-mm) wedges

1½ cups (293 g) uncooked basmati rice, for serving (optional)

Prepare the sauce: In a medium-sized bowl, whisk together the oil, orange juice, teriyaki sauce, honey, red pepper flakes (if using), brown sugar and broth until the sugar dissolves.

Combine the pork, pineapple, bell peppers and red onion in the pot. Pour the sauce over the top. Turn the pot to HIGH pressure, secure the lid, adjust the valve to sealing and set the timer for 20 minutes. When the time is up, do a quick release by turning the valve to venting. Once finished, release the lid.

Meanwhile, if serving with rice, cook according to the package directions.

Remove the pork from the pot and set aside. Stir the cornstarch mixture into the pot until thickened. Serve the pork sliced with the vegetables and sauce over the top with a side of rice (if using).

Eggroll Wonton Bowls

This is a fun—not to mention healthier—take on the classic Chinese side dish. All of the things you love about eggrolls loaded into small but edible cups, keeping this as a classic finger food but in a way that is much easier to make—under pressure for one minute, easy! Using coleslaw mix makes this not only a time-saver but a friend to your budget.

Serves 6

$2.08 per serving

Cooking spray
24 wonton wrappers
2 tsp (10 ml) canola oil
1½ lbs (680 g) ground pork
1 tsp salt
½ tsp freshly ground black pepper
½ tsp garlic powder
½ tsp ground ginger
3 cups (360 g) coleslaw mix
4 green onions, thinly sliced
2 tbsp (30 ml) soy sauce
1 tsp toasted sesame oil
½ cup (120 ml) water
Sweet chili sauce, for serving (optional)

Preheat the oven to 350°F (180°C). Using cooking spray, working in batches, spray the inside of the wells of a muffin pan, place a wonton wrapper in each well and gently push down, forming a cup. Spray the inside of the wonton cups lightly, then bake for 8 to 10 minutes, or until golden brown.

Meanwhile, turn the pot to sauté mode on HIGH until the screen says hot. Add the oil, then the pork, salt and pepper, and cook for 2 to 3 minutes, or until browned. Add the garlic powder and ground ginger, and stir for 30 seconds. Stir in the coleslaw mix, green onions, soy sauce, sesame oil and water. Turn the pot to HIGH pressure, secure the lid, adjust the valve to sealing and set the timer for 1 minute. When the time is up, do a quick release by turning the valve to venting. Once finished, release the lid.

Return the pot to sauté mode on HIGH and continue to cook, stirring, for 5 minutes, or until the liquid has reduced by half. Serve in the wonton cups and top with the sweet chili sauce (if using).

Easy Beef Pho

Pho is a Vietnamese soup known for its savory broth that cooks the meat right in the bowl. It's extraordinarily flavorful with a low ingredient count that will surprise you. I have modified the process slightly to where the meat is precooked in the pot, so no one should be afraid to try it!

Serves 8

$2.41 per serving

2 tbsp (30 ml) canola oil

2 lbs (905 g) shaved beef

1 large onion, quartered

1 (1" [2.5-cm]) piece fresh ginger, sliced

2 (32-oz [946-ml]) containers pho broth

2 tbsp (30 ml) low-sodium soy sauce

8 oz (225 g) rice noodles

1 (14-oz [400-g]) can bean sprouts, drained

Optional Toppings

Fresh cilantro leaves

Sliced jalapeño peppers

Green onions, thinly sliced

Hoisin sauce

Sriracha

Fresh mint leaves

Sliced radishes

Lime wedges

Turn the pot to sauté mode on HIGH until the screen says hot. Add the oil, then the beef, and cook, stirring, for 5 to 7 minutes, or until browned. Remove from the pot and set aside. Add the onion, ginger, broth and soy sauce to the pot. Turn the pot to HIGH pressure, secure the lid, adjust the valve to sealing and set the timer for 5 minutes. When the time is up, do a quick release by turning the valve to venting. Once finished, release the lid.

Meanwhile, cook the noodles according to the package directions.

Carefully remove the onion and ginger from the broth using a slotted spoon. Divide the beef, bean sprouts and noodles evenly among the bowls. Fill each bowl with the broth and top with your desired toppings.

Red Curry Coconut Chicken

If there was ever a cheat recipe that's packed with flavor and takes no effort, this might be the winner. Using store-bought red curry paste —because it's cheaper than making your own— makes this dish so quick to put together, you'll almost feel guilty about how much time you save. Its heat is nicely contrasted by the cool and creamy coconut milk, making it a good fit for even those who don't prefer spicy foods.

Serves 8

$2.38 per serving

2 tbsp (30 ml) canola oil

2 lbs (905 g) boneless, skinless chicken thighs, diced into 1" (2.5-cm) pieces

2 cloves garlic, minced

1 carrot, diagonally sliced

2 tbsp (30 g) red curry paste

1 cup (240 ml) water

1½ cups (293 g) uncooked basmati rice

1 red bell pepper, seeded and sliced into thin, 2" (5-cm)-long strips

1 green bell pepper, seeded and sliced into thin, 2" (5-cm)-long strips

1 lb (455 g) snow peas, ends trimmed

1 (13.5-oz [385-g]) can coconut milk, shaken

2 tbsp (16 g) cornstarch mixed with 2 tbsp (30 ml) water

Turn the pot to sauté mode on HIGH until the screen says hot. Add the oil, then the chicken, and cook for 4 to 5 minutes, or until slightly browned. Stir in the garlic and cook for 1 minute. Add the carrot and cook, stirring, for 2 to 3 minutes. Stir in the curry paste and water. Turn the pot to HIGH pressure, secure the lid, adjust the valve to sealing and set the timer for 8 minutes. When the time is up, do a quick release by turning the valve to venting. Once finished, release the lid.

Meanwhile, cook the rice according to the package directions.

Turn the pot to sauté mode on HIGH. Stir in the bell peppers, snow peas and coconut milk, and cook for 5 minutes, or until the peppers begin to soften. Stir in the cornstarch mixture until thickened. Serve over the rice.

Sweet and Spicy Glazed Salmon

If you cook salmon often, it can be easy to fall into a rut. The few but flavorful ingredients here make a simple glaze; made with only honey, soy sauce, brown sugar and Sriracha, it takes ordinary salmon and turns it into an exciting meal worthy of dinner guests—or your family. Sriracha does add a little kick, so be sparing if you don't enjoy food with heat.

Serves 6

$2.19 per serving

1½ cups (293 g) uncooked basmati rice, for serving (optional)

2 lb (905 g) salmon fillet, cut into 6 fillets, thawed if frozen

1 tsp salt

½ tsp freshly ground black pepper

1 cup (240 ml) water

⅓ cup (115 g) honey

⅓ cup (75 g) light brown sugar

¼ cup (60 ml) soy sauce

1 tsp Sriracha

If serving with rice, cook according to the package directions.

Season the salmon with the salt and pepper. Lay the salmon, skin side down, on a piece of parchment paper, overlapping if necessary. Add the water to the pot. Place the parchment on the trivet and place it in the pot. Turn the pot to HIGH pressure, secure the lid, adjust the valve to sealing and set the timer for 5 minutes. When the time is up, do a quick release by turning the valve to venting. Once finished, release the lid.

Meanwhile, in a small pan over medium heat, combine the honey, brown sugar, soy sauce and Sriracha, and heat, stirring constantly, until the mixture reaches a boil, then immediately remove from the heat.

Serve the sauce over the salmon with a side of rice (if using).

Fiesta Faves

Any skeptic that thinks you can't reproduce these authentic recipes in an Instant Pot is in for a big surprise! Loaded with recipes you likely had no idea could be made this easily, this chapter also explores a few techniques that deliver maximum flavor to every dish. Dedicated to any meal with Latin inspiration, these Latin-inspired recipes work great for your budget and come together with minimal effort. This is one of my favorite types of cuisines to eat, as it always saves me money while also serving up a flavor profile more unique than an average weeknight meal. From crispy carnitas (page 111) to verde posole (page 116), we're exploring a whole new world of flavors for you to try in your kitchen without breaking the bank!

Green Chile Chicken Enchilada Casserole

Like lasagna, these layered cheesy enchiladas come together in less time and taste just as good as any Mexican restaurant's you can find! Making them at home makes them better on your budget, and frankly, much more flavorful.

Serves 8

$1.74 per serving

3 lbs (1.4 kg) boneless, skinless chicken thighs

2 tsp (12 g) salt

1 tsp freshly ground black pepper

2 tbsp (30 ml) canola oil

1 medium-sized onion, diced

6 cloves garlic, minced

1 (28-oz [828-ml]) can green chile enchilada sauce, divided

1 (4-oz [115-g]) can diced green chiles

1 (8-oz [225-g]) package cream cheese, softened

20 to 24 corn tortillas

2 cups (230 g) shredded Colby Jack cheese

Optional Toppings

Sour cream

Diced avocado

Salsa

Fresh cilantro

Preheat the oven to 350°F (180°C). Season the chicken with the salt and black pepper. Turn the pot to sauté mode on HIGH until the screen says hot. Add the oil, then the onion, and cook for 5 to 7 minutes, or until translucent. Add the garlic and cook for 1 minute. Stir in 1 cup (240 ml) of the enchilada sauce, then add the chicken. Turn the pot to HIGH pressure, secure the lid, adjust the valve to sealing and set the timer for 10 minutes. When the time is up, do a quick release by turning the valve to venting. Once finished, release the lid.

Remove the chicken from the pot and, using two forks, carefully shred the chicken. Turn the pot to sauté mode on HIGH, and cook the remaining liquid, stirring occasionally, for 6 to 8 minutes, or until reduced by half. Return the chicken to the pot and stir in the green chiles and cream cheese.

Pour ⅓ cup (80 ml) of the remaining enchilada sauce over the bottom of a 9 x 13–inch (23 x 33–cm) baking dish. Layer 6 tortillas in the baking dish, add half of the chicken mixture, 6 more tortillas, and the remaining chicken mixture, and top with the remaining tortillas. Pour the remaining sauce over the top and sprinkle with the cheese. Bake for 15 minutes, or until the cheese is melted and bubbling. Let rest for 10 minutes before serving and serve with your desired toppings.

Red Chile Pork Bites

Tender, spicy and loaded with flavor. Using pork shoulder and some on-hand spices, these pork bites save you money while bringing a little heat with a whole lot of flair. Serve in a burrito or with rice for a pork dinner to make your mouth water.

Serves 6

$1.96 per serving

2 tsp (12 g) salt

1 tsp freshly ground black pepper

1 tbsp (8 g) chili powder

1 tsp ground cumin

1 tsp paprika

3 lb (1.4 kg) boneless pork shoulder, cut into 1" (2.5-cm) pieces

2 tbsp (30 ml) canola oil

1 large onion, diced

4 cloves garlic, minced

1 (10-oz [296-ml]) can red enchilada sauce

Mexican rice, for serving (optional)

Optional Toppings

Fresh lime juice

Fresh cilantro

Tomatoes

Onion

Shredded cheese

Sour cream

In a large bowl, stir together the salt, black pepper, chili powder, cumin and paprika. Toss the pork in the seasoning mixture until fully coated. Turn the pot to sauté mode on HIGH until the screen says hot. Add the oil, then the onion, and cook for 5 to 7 minutes, or until translucent. Add the garlic and cook for 1 minute. Add the pork, then pour in the enchilada sauce and stir to coat. Turn the pot to HIGH pressure, secure the lid, adjust the valve to sealing and set the timer for 50 minutes. When the time is up, do a quick release by turning the valve to venting. Once finished, release the lid.

Serve over Mexican rice (if using) or in a bowl with your favorite toppings. Serve the sauce from the pot over the meat.

Salsa Verde Pork Tacos

If you try nothing else in this book, I beg you to try these pork tacos. Bursting with flavor, a mild kick and loaded with your favorite toppings, these tacos are perfect for taco Tuesday or any day of the week!

Serves 6

$2.39 **per serving**

2 lb (905 g) boneless pork shoulder

1 tsp salt

1 tsp freshly ground black pepper

2 tbsp (30 ml) canola oil

1 large onion, chopped

1 cup (240 ml) chicken broth

1 (16-oz [455-g]) jar salsa verde

12 corn or flour tortillas, toasted or warmed

Optional Toppings

Chopped fresh cilantro

Diced avocado

Lime wedges

Sour cream

Salsa

Season the pork with the salt and pepper. Turn the pot to sauté mode on HIGH until the screen says hot. Add the oil, then the onion, and cook for 5 to 7 minutes, or until softened. Stir in the broth, then add the pork and salsa. Turn the pot to HIGH pressure, secure the lid, adjust the valve to sealing and set the timer for 50 minutes. When the time is up, do a quick release by turning the valve to venting. Once finished, release the lid.

Remove the pork from the pot and, using two forks, carefully shred the pork and return it to the liquid. Serve in tortillas with your choice of toppings.

Simple Chorizo and Bean Tostadas

A fast-food favorite gets a fancy facelift without the high price point. These tostadas are served with fresh cilantro, cheese and a zesty home-made sauce. They are unlike any you've had before, and you'll be clamoring for more!

Serves 6

$1.99 per serving

1 tbsp (15 ml) canola oil
1 medium-sized onion, diced
1 lb (455 g) mild chorizo
1 (15-oz [425-g]) can pinto beans, drained
1 cup (240 ml) chicken broth
12 tostada shells

Sauce
½ cup (115 g) sour cream
¼ tsp salt
1 tsp sugar
1 tbsp (3 g) minced fresh cilantro
Zest of 1 lime
Juice of ½ lime

Toppings
Shredded lettuce
Jack cheese
Fresh cilantro

Turn the pot to sauté mode on HIGH until the screen says hot. Add the oil, then the onion, and cook for 7 to 10 minutes, or until browned. Add the chorizo and cook for 3 to 5 minutes. Stir in the beans and broth. Turn the pot to HIGH pressure, secure the lid, adjust the valve to sealing and set the timer for 5 minutes. When the time is up, do a quick release by turning the valve to venting. Once finished, release the lid.

Meanwhile, prepare the sauce: In a small bowl, stir together the sour cream, salt, sugar, cilantro, lime zest and juice. Set aside.

Turn the pot to sauté mode on HIGH. Mash the beans and cook, stirring constantly, for 5 minutes. Turn off the pot and let rest for 5 minutes. Top the tostada shells with the bean mixture, a drizzle of the sauce, plus lettuce, cheese and cilantro.

Chicken Burrito Bowl

Next time you're craving a burrito bowl, skip the fast-casual chain and try making your own right at home. Packed with all your favorite mix-ins, and your choice of toppings, this bowl has all the flavor, and you'll be saving money at the same time!

Serves 6

$2.45 per serving

2 tsp (12 g) salt

1 tsp freshly ground black pepper

1 tbsp (8 g) chili powder

1 tsp ground cumin

1 tsp garlic powder

1 tsp onion powder

1 tsp paprika

1½ lbs (680 g) boneless, skinless chicken thighs, cut into 1" (2.5-cm) pieces

1 (14.5-oz [429-ml]) can chicken broth

1 (15.5-oz [439-g]) can corn, drained

1 (15.5-oz [439-g]) can black beans, drained

1 cup (260 g) mild or medium salsa

1 (4-oz [115-g]) can diced green chiles

1 cup (195 g) uncooked basmati rice

1 cup (115 g) shredded Mexican blend cheese

1 cup (230 g) sour cream, for topping

2 tbsp (6 g) chopped fresh cilantro leaves

In a medium-sized bowl, stir together the salt, black pepper, chili powder, cumin, garlic powder, onion powder and paprika. Toss the chicken in the seasoning mixture until fully coated.

Combine the broth, corn, beans, salsa and chiles in the pot and stir. Add the chicken and pour the rice on top. Turn the pot to HIGH pressure, secure the lid, adjust the valve to sealing and set the timer for 10 minutes. When the time is up, do a quick release by turning the valve to venting. Once finished, release the lid.

Serve in a bowl topped with the cheese, sour cream and cilantro.

Shredded Beef Nachos

What's better than loaded nachos? Nachos loaded with this shredded beef! You can turn any pile of chips into an extraordinary meal packed with flavor. Don't take my word for it; after testing this recipe, there were zero leftovers!

Serves 6

$2.41 per serving

2 lb (905 g) beef chuck roast

2 tsp (12 g) salt

1 tsp freshly ground black pepper

2 tbsp (30 ml) canola oil

1 medium-sized onion, diced

1 cup (240 ml) water

1 cup (260 g) prepared salsa

1 tsp ground cumin

2 tsp (5 g) chili powder

1 tsp garlic powder

1 tsp onion powder

1 tsp paprika

1 tsp dried oregano

1 (12-oz [340-g]) bag tortilla chips

2 cups (230 g) shredded mild Cheddar cheese

Optional Toppings

Sliced olives

Jalapeño peppers

Sour cream

Salsa

Fresh cilantro

Season the beef with the salt and pepper. Turn the pot to sauté mode on HIGH until the screen says hot. Add the oil and cook the beef for 4 minutes per side, or until browned. Remove from the pot and set aside. Add the onion and cook for 5 to 7 minutes, or until translucent. Stir in the water, salsa, cumin, chili powder, garlic powder, onion powder, paprika and oregano. Return the beef to the pot. Turn the pot to HIGH pressure, secure the lid, adjust the valve to sealing and set the timer for 40 minutes. When the time is up, do a quick release by turning the valve to venting. Once finished, release the lid.

Set the oven to broil on HIGH. Remove the beef from the pot and, using two forks, carefully shred the beef and return it to the liquid. On a parchment-lined baking sheet, arrange the chips and cover with the cheese, then broil for 3 to 5 minutes, or until the cheese is melted. Add the shredded beef to the chips and top with your desired toppings.

Crispy Carnitas with Pickled Onions

A fun riff on classic pork carnitas that uses a little trick to get the tender and crispy edges we all know and love. Finishing in the broiler is the best way to get the perfect amount of crispy edges. Tender pieces of pork are only made better by being piled onto a tortilla with some homemade pickled onions and your favorite toppings!

Serves 6

$2.45 per serving

3 lb (1.4 kg) boneless pork shoulder, cut into 2" (5-cm) pieces

2 tsp (12 g) salt

1 tsp freshly ground black pepper

3 tbsp (45 ml) canola oil

4 cloves garlic, minced

1½ tsp (2 g) dried oregano

1 tsp chili powder

1 tsp paprika

1 tsp onion powder

1 cup (240 ml) water

Juice of ½ orange

3 (2" [5-cm]) strips orange peels

Pickled Onions

½ cup (120 ml) water

¼ cup (60 ml) white vinegar

¼ cup (60 ml) cider vinegar

¼ cup (50 g) sugar

1½ tsp (9 g) salt

1 medium-sized red onion, very thinly sliced

12 corn or flour tortillas, toasted or warmed, for serving

Chopped fresh cilantro, diced avocado, lime wedges or salsa, for serving (optional)

Season the pork with the salt and pepper. Turn the pot to sauté mode on HIGH until the screen says hot. Add the oil, then the pork, working in batches, and cook for 2 to 4 minutes, or until browned on all sides. Stir in the garlic, oregano, chili powder, paprika and onion powder. Add the water, orange juice and orange peels. Turn the pot to HIGH pressure, secure the lid, adjust the valve to sealing and set the timer for 40 minutes. When the time is up, do a quick release by turning the valve to venting. Once finished, release the lid.

Meanwhile, prepare the pickled onions: In a small pan over medium-high heat, combine the water, white vinegar, cider vinegar, sugar and salt. Once the mixture reaches a boil, remove from the heat and add the onion, making sure the onion is fully submerged in the pickling liquid. Stirring occasionally, let cool to room temperature for 20 to 30 minutes before serving.

Set the oven to broil on HIGH. Remove the orange peels from the pot. Transfer the pork to a rimmed baking sheet and, using two forks, carefully shred the pork. Pour ¼ cup (60 ml) of the cooking juices over the pork and place in the oven to broil for 3 to 5 minutes, or until the edges begin to crisp. Turn the pork over, add more cooking juices, if needed, and cook for 3 to 5 minutes more. Serve in tortillas with the pickled onions and your choice of toppings.

Ropa Vieja

A popular Cuban stew, ropa vieja is often seen in many parts of the Caribbean. It is traditionally cooked with flank steak, but I replaced it with beef chuck to make it easy on the budget. It's well known for the long strands of pulled beef and a deeply flavored tomato sauce. If you're looking to change up your dinner routine, this dish is the first one to try.

Serves 6

$2.99 per serving

2 lb (905 g) beef chuck roast

2 tsp (12 g) salt

1 tsp freshly ground black pepper

2 tbsp (30 ml) canola oil, divided

1 large onion, sliced

1 large red bell pepper, seeded and sliced

1 large green bell pepper, seeded and sliced

3 cloves garlic, minced

2 tbsp (32 g) tomato paste

1 tsp ground cumin

1 tsp dried oregano

2 tsp (5 g) paprika

1 cup (240 ml) chicken broth

1 (28-oz [800-g]) can diced tomatoes

1½ cups (293 g) uncooked basmati rice

½ cup (50 g) small Spanish olives (optional)

Season the beef with the salt and black pepper. Turn the pot to sauté mode on HIGH until the screen says hot. Add 1 tablespoon (15 ml) of the oil, then the beef, and cook for 4 minutes per side, or until browned. Remove from the pot and set aside. Add the remaining 1 tablespoon (15 ml) of oil to the pot, then the onion and bell peppers, and cook for 3 to 4 minutes, or until just softened. Stir in the garlic, tomato paste, cumin, oregano and paprika, and cook for 1 minute. Pour in the chicken broth and tomatoes.

Return the beef to the pot. Turn the pot to HIGH pressure, secure the lid, adjust the valve to sealing and set the timer for 40 minutes. When the time is up, do a quick release by turning the valve to venting. Once finished, release the lid.

Meanwhile, cook the rice according to the package directions.

Remove the beef from the pot and, using two forks, carefully shred the beef and return it to the liquid. Add the olives (if using). Turn the pot to sauté mode on HIGH and cook, stirring occasionally, for 10 minutes, or until the sauce begins to thicken slightly. Serve the stew over the rice.

Fish Tacos with Creamy Avocado Sauce

Tilapia is a delicious mild-flavored and cost-effective fish that is the perfect choice for these tacos. Coated with simple seasonings, and topped off with a cool avocado sauce, these tacos make for an excellent high-protein meal that's budget-friendly and satisfying!

Serves 6

$2.14 per serving

4 frozen tilapia fillets, thawed
2 tsp (10 ml) canola oil
2 tsp (12 g) salt
1 tsp freshly ground black pepper
1 tbsp (7 g) paprika
1 tbsp (8 g) chili powder
1 cup (240 ml) water
Juice of 1 lime, divided
12 tortillas, toasted or warmed
2 or 3 cilantro sprigs

Sauce

½ cup (115 g) sour cream
1 ripe avocado, pitted and mashed
2 tbsp (6 g) chopped fresh cilantro
Juice of 1 lime
½ tsp salt
¼ tsp freshly ground black pepper
1 jalapeño pepper, seeded and chopped (optional)

Brush the fish with the oil and season with the salt, pepper, paprika and chili powder. Let sit for 10 minutes.

Meanwhile, prepare the sauce. In a small bowl, stir together the sour cream, avocado, cilantro, lime juice, salt, black pepper and jalapeño (if using). Refrigerate until ready to serve.

Pour 1 cup (240 ml) of water into the pot and place the trivet in the pot with parchment paper on top. Layer the fish onto the parchment-lined trivet. Squeeze half of the lime juice over the fish. Turn the pot to HIGH pressure, secure the lid, adjust the valve to sealing and set the timer for 8 minutes. When the time is up, do a quick release by turning the valve to venting. Once finished, release the lid.

Remove the fish from the pot. Using two forks, flake the fish into 1-inch (2.5-cm) pieces; squeeze the remaining lime juice over the fish. Serve on tortillas, topped with the sauce and cilantro.

Authentic Chicken Verde Posole

Red or green? Posole is a New Mexican staple with the state question, "Red or green?" I give you a green chili chicken posole, made with your choice of chicken or pork and red or green chili. Mild yet flavorful, it's New Mexico's version of the comfort classic, chicken noodle soup.

Serves 6

$1.88 per serving

1½ lbs (680 g) boneless, skinless chicken thighs, cut into ½" (1.3-cm) pieces

1 tsp salt

½ tsp freshly ground black pepper

2 tbsp (30 ml) canola oil

1 jalapeño pepper, seeded and finely diced

4 cloves garlic, minced

1 tsp chili powder

1 tsp dried oregano

1 tsp ground cumin

2 (15.5-oz [439-g]) cans white hominy, drained

1 (16-oz [455-g]) jar green salsa verde

1 (32-oz [946-ml]) container chicken broth

Optional Toppings

Lime wedges

Cotija cheese

Fresh cilantro

Avocado

Jalapeño pepper

Season the chicken with the salt and pepper. Turn the pot to sauté mode on HIGH until the screen says hot. Add the oil, then the chicken, and cook for 5 minutes, or until browned on all sides. Stir in the jalapeño and garlic, and cook for 1 minute. Add the chili powder, oregano and cumin, and cook, stirring, for 1 minute. Stir in the hominy, salsa and broth.

Turn the pot to HIGH pressure, secure the lid, adjust the valve to sealing and set the timer for 20 minutes. When the time is up, do a quick release by turning the valve to venting. Once finished, release the lid.

Serve with your choice of toppings.

Cup of Cozy

Soups are easily some of my favorite things to make, but the idea of making them in the Instant Pot makes them even more appealing, not to mention a lot easier. There are so many varieties of soups available, from the hearty meat and veggie filled to the creamy and richly flavored. This chapter doesn't hold back on any of them! It's almost impossible to get bored with making soup, and I made sure you have plenty of variety to choose from, all of which are both delicious and satisfying. They are possibly the ultimate budget-friendly meal when you really think about it, keeping your tummy and your wallet full!

Baked Potato Soup

This is all of your favorite things about a baked potato made into one showstopping soup. It makes the perfect meal when you don't want to break the bank on dinner or are pressed for time. Potatoes are a great bang for your buck when making frugal dishes, and they are super filling. This soup is flavor packed all on its own, but who doesn't love some toppings? Choose your favorites, load it up and enjoy!

Serves 6

$1.42 per serving

3 tbsp (45 ml) canola oil

3 tbsp (42 g) unsalted butter

1 large onion, diced

1 clove garlic, minced

6 cups (1.4 L) chicken broth

3 lbs (1.4 kg) russet potatoes, peeled and quartered

½ cup (120 ml) heavy cream

4 oz (115 g) cream cheese

2 cups (230 g) shredded medium Cheddar cheese

1 tsp salt

2 tsp (5 g) freshly ground black pepper

2 tbsp (16 g) cornstarch mixed with 2 tbsp (30 ml) water

Optional Toppings

Shredded mild Cheddar cheese

Chopped cooked bacon

Sour cream

Fresh chives

Turn the pot to sauté mode on HIGH until the screen says hot. Add the oil and butter. Once the butter has melted, add the onion, and cook for 5 to 7 minutes, or until softened and translucent.

Stir in the garlic and broth. Add the potatoes to the pot. Turn the pot to HIGH pressure, secure the lid, adjust the valve to sealing and set the timer for 8 minutes. When the time is up, do a quick release by turning the valve to venting. Once finished, release the lid.

Turn the pot to sauté mode on HIGH. Gently mash the potatoes in the pot and cook for about 10 minutes. Stir in the cream, cream cheese, Cheddar, salt and pepper, and cook for 2 to 3 minutes, or until the cheese is fully melted. Stir in the cornstarch mixture until thickened.

Serve topped with your choice of toppings.

One-Pot Lasagna Soup

This soup is a fun twist on an Italian classic, and much easier to prepare. All your favorite lasagna ingredients come together to make this rich and flavorful soup, packed with ground beef and pasta, two budget-friendly superheroes. You'll be so pleased with this quick dinner, it will become your new comfort food favorite.

Serves 6

$2.21 per serving

2 tbsp (30 ml) canola oil

1 large onion, diced

1 lb (455 g) ground beef

1 tsp salt

½ tsp freshly ground black pepper

2 tbsp (32 g) tomato paste

1 (32-oz [946-ml]) container chicken broth

3 cloves garlic, minced

1 (28-oz [800-g]) can crushed tomatoes

1 tsp dried oregano

½ tsp dried thyme

½ (16-oz [455-g]) package lasagna noodles, broken into bite-size pieces

1 cup (246 g) ricotta cheese

2 cups (230 g) shredded mozzarella cheese

Turn the pot to sauté mode on HIGH until the screen says hot. Add the oil, then the onion, and cook for 4 minutes, or until just softened. Add the ground beef, salt and pepper, and cook for 5 to 7 minutes, or until no longer pink. Stir in the tomato paste.

Stir in the broth, garlic, tomatoes, oregano, thyme and lasagna noodles. Turn the pot to HIGH pressure, secure the lid, adjust the valve to sealing and set the timer for 15 minutes. When the time is up, do a quick release by turning the valve to venting. Once finished, release the lid.

Serve in bowls topped with ricotta and mozzarella.

Traditional Italian Minestrone Soup

This Italian favorite comes in many forms. This is the most traditional version, which to me is best and has the most well-developed flavors. Although no recipe looks exactly like another because there is truly no set recipe for this soup, it's what I like to call a "use it up" recipe. You can throw in leftover vegetables, maybe some meat, whatever noodles you have on hand, and voilà! Dinner is done.

Serves 6

$2.66 per serving

3 tbsp (45 ml) canola oil

1 medium-sized onion, chopped

2 carrots, peeled and chopped

2 celery ribs, chopped

2 zucchini, chopped

¼ cup (65 g) tomato paste

1 (32-oz [946-ml]) container chicken broth

1 (32-oz [946-ml]) container beef broth

1 (15-oz [425-g]) can white kidney beans, drained

1 (28-oz [800-g]) can diced tomatoes

4 cloves garlic, minced

2 tsp (1 g) dried parsley

1 tsp salt

¼ tsp freshly ground black pepper

1 cup (105 g) uncooked short pasta, such as ditalini

⅓ cup (33 g) grated Parmesan cheese

1 (15-oz [425-g]) can chickpeas, drained

½ cup (20 g) chopped fresh basil

1 cup (240 ml) half-and-half

Turn the pot to sauté mode on HIGH until the screen says hot. Add the oil, then the onion, carrots, celery and zucchini, and cook for 5 to 7 minutes, or until softened. Stir in the tomato paste.

Add the chicken broth, beef broth, kidney beans, tomatoes, garlic, parsley, salt, pepper, pasta, Parmesan and chickpeas. Turn the pot to HIGH pressure, secure the lid, adjust the valve to sealing and set the timer for 15 minutes. When the time is up, do a quick release by turning the valve to venting. Once finished, release the lid.

Stir in the basil and half-and-half, then serve.

Butternut Squash Soup

Rich, creamy and vibrantly colored, there's something cozy about this squash soup. It comes together with minimal effort and maximum flavor. Its low ingredient count helps when you are staying frugal minded. You might notice that I don't remove the squash skin. I know this may sound crazy, but it's actually edible, and knowing so makes it not worth the extra effort of removing it!

Serves 6

$1.32 per serving

1 tbsp (15 ml) canola oil

1 large onion, diced

1 tsp dried thyme

1 tsp salt

½ tsp freshly ground black pepper

1 (3-lb [1.4-kg]) butternut squash, chopped into 2" (5-cm) cubes

1 (32-oz [946-ml]) container chicken broth

Fried onions, for topping (optional)

Turn the pot to sauté mode on HIGH until the screen says hot. Add the oil, then the onion, and cook for 10 to 15 minutes, or until browned and starting to caramelize. Add the thyme, salt and pepper, and cook, stirring, for 1 minute. Add the squash and broth. Turn the pot to HIGH pressure, secure the lid, adjust the valve to sealing and set the timer for 20 minutes. When the time is up, do a quick release by turning the valve to venting. Once finished, release the lid.

Working in batches, transfer the mixture to a blender, cover the blender with a towel, or close and leave the easy-pour spout open for the steam to escape. Blend until smooth and creamy. Serve topped with fried onions (if using).

French Onion Soup

This rich-flavored soup is what a budget recipe is all about. The deep flavors come from cooking the onions to the point of caramelization before it goes under pressure, a slightly time-consuming but necessary step. The results are an onion-filled, beefy, slightly sweet broth, topped with toasty bread and melty cheese. This is a soup that will have you coming back for seconds.

Serves 6

$1.67 per serving

½ cup (112 g/1 stick) unsalted butter

3 tbsp (45 ml) canola oil

3 lbs (1.4 kg) sweet onions, thinly sliced

½ tsp sugar

1 tsp salt

1 tsp freshly ground black pepper

1 tsp dried thyme

2 (32-oz [946-ml]) containers beef broth

1 tbsp (8 g) cornstarch mixed with 1 tbsp (15 ml) water

1 baguette, sliced and toasted

3 cups (345 g) shredded mozzarella cheese

Turn the pot to sauté mode on HIGH until the screen says hot. Add the butter and oil. Once the butter has melted, add the onions and sugar, and cook, stirring occasionally, for 25 to 30 minutes, or until the onions are caramelized to a dark golden brown. Stir in the salt, pepper and thyme, and cook for 1 minute. Stir in the broth. Turn the pot to HIGH pressure, secure the lid, adjust the valve to sealing and set the timer for 15 minutes. When the time is up, do a quick release by turning the valve to venting. Once finished, release the lid.

Stir in the cornstarch mixture until slightly thickened. Set the oven to broil on HIGH. Ladle the soup into six oven-safe bowls, then top with the baguette slices and cheese. Place the bowls on a baking sheet and broil for 3 to 5 minutes, until the cheese is melted, bubbly and browning. Allow the soup to cool for 5 minutes before serving.

Creamy Chicken with Dumplings

This is a fun twist on a fan favorite, but it's not your standard chicken and dumplings. This soup's creamy base is rich and flavorful. Accompanied by soft, homemade dumplings, simple ingredients come together to make this a true one-of-a-kind soup.

Serves 6

$2.08 per serving

1½ lbs (680 g) boneless, skinless chicken thighs

1 tsp salt

½ tsp freshly ground black pepper

2 tbsp (30 ml) canola oil

1 medium-sized onion, diced

2 celery ribs, diced

3 carrots, shredded

2 cloves garlic, minced

1 (14.5-oz [429-ml]) can chicken broth

1 tsp dried thyme

2 cups (475 ml) heavy cream

3 tbsp (24 g) cornstarch, mixed with 3 tbsp (45 ml) water

1 cup (30 g) baby spinach leaves

Dumplings

1 cup (125 g) all-purpose flour, plus more for dusting

1 tsp baking powder

½ tsp salt

1 large egg

1 tbsp (15 ml) water

Season the chicken with the salt and pepper. Turn the pot to sauté mode on HIGH until the screen says hot. Add the oil, then the onion, celery and carrots, and cook for 5 to 7 minutes, or until the onion is translucent. Add the garlic and cook, stirring, for 1 minute.

Stir in the chicken broth and thyme. Add the chicken to the pot. Turn the pot to HIGH pressure, secure the lid, adjust the valve to sealing and set the timer for 10 minutes. When the time is up, do a quick release by turning the valve to venting. Once finished, release the lid.

Meanwhile, prepare the dumplings: In a small bowl, combine the flour, baking powder, salt, egg and water. Slowly mix together until a dough forms. Using your hands, knead the dough on a floured surface for 2 to 3 minutes, adding more flour as needed until a dough is formed that isn't sticky. Then roll out the dough into a long rope. Cut into ¼-inch (6-mm) pieces or smaller.

Remove the chicken from the pot and, using two forks, carefully shred the chicken and return it to the liquid. Turn the pot to sauté mode on HIGH. Stir in the dumplings and cook for 3 minutes, stirring occasionally. Slowly stir in the cream, then stir in the cornstarch mixture until thickened. Add the baby spinach, and stir until wilted.

Tomato Pork Stew

There's something about stews that is just so satisfying. In this recipe, hearty pieces of budget-friendly pork shoulder are bathed in a rich tomato stew. Perfect served over pasta, it's hard to have just one bowl! The canned tomatoes and pasta help to keep this stew affordable.

Serves 6

$2.32 per serving

2 lb (905 g) boneless pork shoulder, cut into 1" (2.5-cm) pieces

2 tsp (12 g) salt

1 tsp freshly ground black pepper

2 tbsp (30 ml) canola oil, divided

1 large onion, diced

2 cloves garlic, minced

1 tsp onion powder

2 tsp (2 g) dried oregano

1 (28-oz [800-g]) can stewed tomatoes, crushed or diced

1 (14.5-oz [429-ml]) can chicken broth

1 (1-lb [455-g]) package rotini pasta

3 tbsp (24 g) cornstarch mixed with 3 tbsp (45 ml) water

Season the pork with the salt and pepper. Turn the pot to sauté mode on HIGH until the screen says hot. Add 1 tablespoon (15 ml) of the oil, then the pork, and cook for 10 minutes, or until browned on all sides. Remove from the pot and set aside. Add the remaining tablespoon (15 ml) of oil to the pot, then the onion, and cook for 5 to 7 minutes, or until translucent. Stir in the garlic, onion powder and oregano. Add the tomatoes and stir in the broth. Return the pork to the pot. Turn the pot to HIGH pressure, secure the lid, adjust the valve to sealing and set the timer for 40 minutes. When the time is up, do a quick release by turning the valve to venting. Once finished, release the lid.

Meanwhile, cook the pasta according to the package directions.

Stir the cornstarch mixture into the stew until thickened. Serve over the pasta.

Yellow Split Pea Soup

The yellow peas in this soup are a beautiful golden-hued cousin to the traditional ones used in split pea soup, but with a slightly sweet and milder flavor. Starting with dried peas to save money, this recipe comes together with little effort, and the results are an outstanding yet simple soup that'll leave you satisfied.

Serves 6

$1.02 per serving

1 tbsp (15 ml) canola oil
1 large onion, diced
1 carrot, diced
1 bay leaf
¼ tsp freshly ground black pepper
2½ cups (493 g) dried yellow split peas
1 (32-oz [946-ml]) container chicken broth
4 cups (946 ml) water
¼ cup (15 g) chopped fresh parsley or dill

Turn the pot to sauté mode on HIGH until the screen says hot. Add the oil, then the onion, and cook for 10 to 12 minutes, or until browned.

Add the carrot, bay leaf, pepper, peas, broth and water. Turn the pot to HIGH pressure, secure the lid, adjust the valve to sealing and set the timer for 60 minutes. When the time is up, do a quick release by turning the valve to venting. Once finished, release the lid and remove the bay leaf.

Transfer half of the soup to a blender; cover the blender with a towel or close and leave the easy-pour spout open, for the steam to escape. Blend until smooth. Return the blended soup back to the pot and stir. Serve with fresh parsley or dill on top.

Creamy Chicken and Mushroom Soup

A little reminiscent of chicken marsala but in the form of a creamy soup. Saving you money by using chicken thighs, it's a perfect hearty meal for all mushroom lovers!

Serves 6

$2.57 per serving

1 tbsp (15 ml) canola oil

2 tbsp (28 g) unsalted butter

3 cloves garlic, minced

1 lb (455 g) button mushrooms, sliced

1 medium-sized onion, diced

3 carrots, diced

2 celery ribs, diced

1 tsp salt

½ tsp freshly ground black pepper

1 (32-oz [946-ml]) container chicken broth

½ tsp dried thyme

1 bay leaf

1½ lbs (680 g) boneless, skinless chicken thighs, cut into 1" (2.5-cm) pieces

½ cup (120 ml) half-and-half

¼ cup (32 g) cornstarch, mixed with ¼ cup (60 ml) water

2 tbsp (8 g) chopped fresh parsley leaves, for serving

Turn the pot to sauté mode on HIGH until the screen says hot. Add the oil and butter, then the garlic, mushrooms, onion, carrots, celery, salt and pepper, and cook for 5 to 7 minutes, or until softened. Stir in the broth, thyme and bay leaf. Add the chicken. Turn the pot to HIGH pressure, secure the lid, adjust the valve to sealing and set the timer for 7 minutes. When the time is up, do a quick release by turning the valve to venting. Once finished, release the lid.

Remove the bay leaf and chicken from the pot and, using two forks, carefully shred the chicken and return it to the liquid. Stir in the half-and-half and the cornstarch mixture until thickened. Serve topped with the parsley.

Tuscan Ravioli Soup

A rich tomato base, Italian sausage and ravioli—does it get any better than that? This hearty soup has all the makings of a dinnertime staple, and in just a few easy steps. Dinner is on the table in no time at all!

Serves 6

$2.80 per serving

2 tbsp (30 ml) canola oil

1 medium-sized onion, diced

3 cloves garlic, minced

1 lb (455 g) ground Italian sausage

1 tsp salt

½ tsp freshly ground black pepper

1 tsp onion powder

1 tsp garlic powder

1 tsp dried oregano

1 (28-oz [800-g]) can stewed tomatoes

1 (14.5-oz [429-ml]) can chicken broth

1 (20-oz [567-g]) package frozen mini cheese ravioli

½ cup (50 g) grated Parmesan cheese, plus more for serving

1 cup (240 ml) half-and-half

4 cups (120 g) baby spinach leaves

Turn the pot to sauté mode on HIGH until the screen says hot. Add the oil, then the onion and garlic, and cook for 3 to 5 minutes, or until just softened. Add the sausage, salt, pepper, onion powder, garlic powder and oregano, and cook for 5 to 7 minutes, or until the sausage is no longer pink. Stir in the tomatoes, broth and ravioli. Turn the pot to HIGH pressure, secure the lid, adjust the valve to sealing and set the timer for 10 minutes. When the time is up, do a quick release by turning the valve to venting. Once finished, release the lid.

Stir in the Parmesan, half-and-half and spinach, until the spinach is wilted. Serve topped with additional Parmesan.

Kielbasa and Navy Bean Soup

This soup is the answer to when you need dinner in a pinch. The filling and extremely budget-friendly navy beans make this a wallet saver. It comes together quickly, and the results are so flavorful you may just feel guilty about how easy it is—I promise you won't actually feel guilty!

Serves 6

$1.30 per serving

1 tbsp (15 ml) canola oil

14 oz (400 g) kielbasa, sliced into ½" (1.3-cm) coins

6 cloves garlic, minced

1 (32-oz [946-ml]) container chicken broth

1 bay leaf

4 (15.5-oz [439-g]) cans navy beans, drained

1 tsp hot sauce (optional)

1 bunch kale, stemmed and finely chopped or shredded (about 5 cups [335 g])

Grated Parmesan cheese, for garnish

Turn the pot to sauté mode on HIGH until the screen says hot. Add the oil, then the kielbasa, and cook for 4 to 6 minutes, or until browned on both sides. Add the garlic and cook for 1 minute. Stir in the broth, bay leaf and beans. Turn the pot to HIGH pressure, secure the lid, adjust the valve to sealing and set the timer for 10 minutes. When the time is up, do a quick release by turning the valve to venting. Once finished, release the lid and remove the bay leaf.

Stir in the hot sauce (if using) and kale until wilted. Serve with grated Parmesan on top.

Shredded Chicken Taco Soup

With all of the flavors of shredded chicken tacos, this soup is a fiesta in a bowl. It comes together with minimal effort and deep flavors, and keeps costs low with the chicken and canned goods, making this a true quick-fix meal for busy weeknights. What's not to love about that?!

Serves 8

$1.45 per serving

3 tbsp (45 ml) canola oil

1 large onion, diced

2 cloves garlic, minced

2 tsp (12 g) salt

1 tsp freshly ground black pepper

1 tbsp (8 g) chili powder

1 tsp ground cumin

1 tsp garlic powder

1 tsp onion powder

1 tsp paprika

1 (15.5-oz [439-g]) can black beans, drained

1 (15-oz [425-g]) can corn, drained

2 (10-oz [280-g]) cans diced tomatoes with green chiles

1 (32-oz [946-ml]) container chicken broth

2 lbs (905 g) boneless, skinless chicken thighs

¼ cup (32 g) cornstarch mixed with ¼ cup (60 ml) water

Optional Toppings

2 limes, cut into wedges

Chopped fresh cilantro

Diced avocado

Shredded cheese

Sour cream

Turn the pot to sauté mode on HIGH until the screen says hot. Add the oil, then the onion, and cook for 5 to 7 minutes, or until translucent. Add the garlic and cook for 1 minute. Add the salt, pepper, chili powder, cumin, garlic powder, onion powder and paprika to the pot, and cook, stirring, for 1 minute. Add the beans, corn, tomatoes, broth and chicken. Turn the pot to HIGH pressure, secure the lid, adjust the valve to sealing and set the timer for 12 minutes. When the time is up, do a quick release by turning the valve to venting. Once finished, release the lid.

Remove the chicken from the pot and, using two forks, carefully shred the chicken and return it to the liquid. Stir in the cornstarch mixture until thickened. Serve with your favorite toppings.

Creamy Broccoli Cheddar Soup

Cream-based soups aren't always easy on the budget, but I couldn't imagine not having this one. So, I made it more affordable! Using chicken broth and cornstarch to make it creamy offers two shortcuts: It makes it work better for the Instant Pot and eliminates the need for often-expensive heavy cream—making it cheaper and healthier!

Serves 6

$1.54 per serving

¼ cup (60 ml) canola oil

1 medium-sized onion, diced

2 celery ribs, minced

2 carrots, minced

2 cloves garlic, minced

2 heads broccoli, cut into florets (about 5 cups [455 g])

3 cups (710 ml) chicken broth

3 cups (345 g) shredded medium Cheddar cheese

1 cup (240 ml) milk

1 tsp salt

½ tsp freshly ground black pepper

¼ cup (32 g) cornstarch mixed with ¼ cup (60 ml) water

Turn the pot to sauté mode on HIGH until the screen says hot. Add the oil, then the onion, celery, carrots and garlic, and cook for 8 to 10 minutes, or until the onion begins to brown.

Add the broccoli and broth. Turn the pot to HIGH pressure, secure the lid, adjust the valve to sealing and set the timer for 5 minutes. When the time is up, do a quick release by turning the valve to venting. Once finished, release the lid.

Stir in the Cheddar, 1 cup (115 g) at a time, allowing it to melt completely after each addition. Stir in the milk, salt and pepper, then the cornstarch mixture until thickened. Serve immediately.

Lean Chicken and Bean Chili

If you don't think you can use anything besides ground beef in chili, this recipe will challenge you. It's so flavorful, no one will even notice you made a healthier change with chicken instead of beef! Canned goods are already great on the budget, and you can take that further by stocking up ahead of time when you find them on sale, making this chili a double money saver and almost a complete pantry meal.

Serves 6

$1.83 per serving

2 lbs (905 g) ground chicken

2 tsp (12 g) salt, divided

1½ tsp (4 g) freshly ground black pepper, divided

2 tbsp (30 ml) canola oil

1 green bell pepper, seeded and diced

1 medium-sized onion, diced

2 (15.5-oz [439-g]) cans kidney beans, drained

2 (15.5-oz [439-g]) cans pinto beans, drained

1 (28-oz [800-g]) can crushed tomatoes

1 (28-oz [828-ml]) can tomato sauce

1 (6-oz [170-g]) can tomato paste

2 cups (475 ml) water

1 tbsp (8 g) chili powder

2 tsp (2 g) oregano

1 tsp onion powder

1 tsp garlic powder

1 tsp ground cumin

1 tsp paprika

Season the chicken with 1 teaspoon each of the salt and black pepper. Turn the pot to sauté mode on HIGH until the screen says hot. Add the oil, then the chicken, and cook for 10 to 15 minutes, or until opaque.

Stir in the bell pepper, onion, kidney beans, pinto beans, crushed tomatoes, tomato sauce, tomato paste, water, chili powder, remaining teaspoon of salt, remaining ½ teaspoon of black pepper, oregano, onion powder, garlic powder, cumin and paprika until fully combined. Turn the pot to HIGH pressure, secure the lid, adjust the valve to sealing and set the timer for 30 minutes. When the time is up, do a quick release by turning the valve to venting. Once finished, release the lid.

Let sit for 10 minutes and stir before serving.

Veg Out

Vegetarian meals can come in all sorts of fixings and flavors. This chapter explores a few destinations around the globe that ensure dinner will be anything but boring. From pasta to soups and chilis, every meal is hearty and satisfying; everyone will love these vegetarian delights. While vegetables are naturally cheaper than meat, these recipes are packed with nutrition and you will be saving money with every recipe. So, don't be afraid to explore a different way of cooking and eating; you just might be surprised how good vegetarian food can taste and cost!

Garden Vegetable Primavera

Loaded with vegetables, this vegetarian pasta won't leave meat eaters feeling deprived. This is incredibly versatile, so feel free to swap in any of your favorite vegetables and make this recipe your own. Inexpensive pasta and seasonal vegetables make this one of the cheapest pasta dishes you can make.

Serves 4

$2.77 **per serving**

2 tbsp (30 ml) canola oil

1 head broccoli, cut into florets

2 carrots, sliced

1 medium-sized onion, chopped

1 red bell pepper, seeded and chopped

4 cloves garlic, minced

1 tbsp (6 g) Italian seasoning

1 (32-oz [946-ml]) container chicken broth

1 (1-lb [455-g]) package penne pasta

1 tsp salt

Juice of 1 lemon

1 cup (100 g) grated Parmesan cheese

4 oz (115 g) cherry tomatoes, halved

Fresh basil, sliced, for garnish

Turn the pot to sauté mode on HIGH until the screen says hot. Add the oil, then the broccoli, carrots, onion and bell pepper, and cook for 5 to 7 minutes, or until the onion is softened and translucent. Stir in the garlic and Italian seasoning, and cook for 2 to 3 minutes. Remove from the pot and set aside. Add the broth, pasta and salt to the pot. Turn the pot to HIGH pressure, secure the lid, adjust the valve to sealing and set the timer for 6 minutes. When the time is up, do a quick release by turning the valve to venting. Once finished, release the lid.

Turn the pot to sauté mode on HIGH to cook down any excess liquid from the pot. Return the vegetables to the pot, then stir in the lemon juice, Parmesan and tomatoes, tossing carefully until the Parmesan is just melted. Top with basil to serve.

Cream of Mushroom and Wild Rice Soup

A vegetarian-friendly soup that's as equally satisfying as it is delicious! This soup does not skimp on the mushrooms, using two different varieties. The dried shiitakes are used to make a mushroom broth that really sets this soup apart from the rest. Cooked with wild rice and finished with sour cream, this is not your mom's cream of mushroom soup!

Serves 6

$2.98 per serving

1 (1-oz [28-g]) package dried shiitake mushrooms

2 cups (475 ml) boiling water

3 tbsp (45 ml) canola oil

2 celery ribs, diced

2 carrots, diced

1 medium-sized onion, finely chopped

3 cloves garlic, minced

1 lb (455 g) white mushrooms, sliced

1 tsp salt

½ tsp freshly ground black pepper

1 tsp dried thyme

⅓ cup (80 ml) vermouth or white wine

1 (32-oz [946-ml]) container vegetable broth

1 (6-oz [170-g]) package long-grain and wild rice mix

¼ cup (32 g) cornstarch, mixed with ¼ cup (60 ml) water

1 cup (230 g) sour cream

Place the dried mushrooms in a heatproof bowl and pour the boiling water over them, allowing them to steep for 30 minutes. Strain the water to remove any dirt from the liquid. In a blender, blend the mushrooms with the liquid and set aside.

Turn the pot to sauté mode on HIGH until the screen says hot. Add the oil, then the celery, carrots, onion and garlic, and cook for 5 to 7 minutes, or until they begin to soften. Add the white mushrooms and cook until softened, about 5 minutes; season with the salt, pepper and thyme.

Stir in the vermouth and cook for about 3 minutes to reduce. Stir in the broth and blended mushrooms. Pour the rice on top. Turn the pot to HIGH pressure, secure the lid, adjust the valve to sealing and set the timer for 10 minutes. When the time is up, do a quick release by turning the valve to venting. Once finished, release the lid.

Stir in the cornstarch mixture until thickened, then the sour cream, and serve.

Spicy Tomato Lentil Chili

What's more perfect than chili on a cold night in? With just a few tweaks, this lentil chili is a delicious substitute for vegetarians. Even if you're not vegetarian, you won't be missing the meat here. Lentils make a great swap for ground meat and are even better on the budget!

Serves 4

$2.24 per serving

2 tbsp (30 ml) canola oil
1 large onion, chopped
2 carrots, chopped
1 green bell pepper, seeded and chopped
1 jalapeño pepper, seeded and diced
4 cloves garlic, minced
1½ tbsp (11 g) chili powder
1 tbsp (7 g) ground cumin
½ tsp onion powder
1 tsp dried oregano
½ tsp salt
2 tbsp (32 g) tomato paste
1 (15.5-oz [439-g]) can black beans, drained
2 (14.5-oz [411-g]) cans fire-roasted diced tomatoes
2 cups (384 g) dried brown or green lentils
1 (32-oz [946-ml]) container vegetable broth
1 cup (240 ml) water
1 bunch cilantro, chopped, for serving

Turn the pot to sauté mode on HIGH until it says hot. Add the oil, then the onion, carrots, bell pepper and jalapeño, and cook for 5 to 7 minutes, or until softened. Stir in the garlic, chili powder, cumin, onion powder, oregano, salt and tomato paste, and cook for 1 minute.

Stir in the beans, tomatoes, lentils, broth and 1 cup (240 ml) of water. Turn the pot to HIGH pressure, secure the lid, adjust the valve to sealing and set the timer for 30 minutes. When the time is up, do a quick release by turning the valve to venting. Once finished, release the lid. Serve with cilantro on top.

Creamy Roasted Cauliflower Soup

Personally, I found it hard to believe that the humble and budget-friendly cauliflower could turn into an extraordinarily creamy and flavorful soup. But, I'll be the first to admit I was very wrong! Using your broiler to lightly char the cauliflower adds an overall subtly sweet flavor; it's a simple but vital step to get the most flavor into this soup. The Instant Pot cooks the cauliflower perfectly tender, so everything blends into a velvety smooth, creamy soup.

Serves 6

$1.54 per serving

2 heads cauliflower, cut into bite-size florets
3 tbsp (45 ml) canola oil, divided
1 tsp salt
½ tsp freshly ground black pepper
1 medium-sized red onion, chopped
2 cloves garlic, minced
2 (32-oz [946-ml]) containers vegetable broth
¼ cup (55 g/½ stick) butter
1 tbsp (15 ml) fresh lemon juice
⅛ tsp ground nutmeg
1 green onion, thinly sliced, for serving

Set the oven to broil on HIGH. On a rimmed baking sheet, toss the cauliflower with 2 tablespoons (30 ml) of the oil. Arrange in a single layer and season with the salt and pepper. Place in the oven and broil for 10 to 15 minutes, or until the edges begin to brown, tossing halfway through.

Meanwhile, turn the pot to sauté mode on HIGH until the screen says hot. Add the remaining tablespoon (15 ml) of oil, then the red onion, and cook for 5 to 7 minutes, or until softened and translucent. Stir in the garlic and cook for 1 to 2 minutes.

Reserve 12 florets from the baking sheet. Add the broth and remaining cauliflower to the pot. Turn the pot to HIGH pressure, secure the lid, adjust the valve to sealing and set the timer for 10 minutes. When the time is up, do a quick release by turning the valve to venting. Once finished, release the lid.

Working in batches, transfer the mixture to a blender. Add the butter, lemon juice and nutmeg; cover the blender with a towel or close and leave the easy-pour spout open, for the steam to escape. Blend the mixture until smooth. Top each individual bowl of soup with 2 roasted cauliflower florets and green onion.

Spring Vegetable Pasta with Pine Nuts

In this recipe, fresh springtime vegetables are turned into a quick, simple and flavorful pasta. This dish is a bright and nutritious meal, topped with toasted pine nuts for a fun texture combination.

Serves 6

$2.42 per serving

1 tbsp (15 ml) canola oil

1 shallot, diced

1 bunch asparagus, chopped

2 small zucchini, chopped

1 small yellow summer squash, chopped

3 cloves garlic, minced

1 tsp salt

½ tsp freshly ground black pepper

1 (1-lb [455-g]) package bowtie pasta

1 (32-oz [946-ml]) container vegetable broth

1 (2-oz [55-g]) package pine nuts

Zest and juice of 1 lemon

4 cups (120 g) spinach

1 cup (100 g) grated Parmesan cheese

Turn the pot to sauté mode on HIGH until the screen says hot. Add the oil, then the shallot, and cook for 2 minutes. Add the asparagus, zucchini and squash, and cook for 4 to 5 minutes. Add the garlic, salt and pepper, and cook for 1 minute. Remove the vegetables from the pot and set aside. Add the pasta and broth to the pot. Turn the pot to HIGH pressure, secure the lid, adjust the valve to sealing and set the timer for 6 minutes. When the time is up, do a quick release by turning the valve to venting. Once finished, release the lid.

Meanwhile, in a pan over medium heat, heat the pine nuts for 5 minutes, watching and tossing constantly until toasted with a nutty aroma. Remove from the heat and set aside.

Turn the pot to sauté mode on HIGH to cook down any excess liquid from the pot. Return the vegetables to the pot, then stir in the lemon zest and juice, spinach and Parmesan, until the spinach is just wilted. Serve topped with the pine nuts.

Mediterranean Lentil Soup

Simple and flavorful, this soup is a great meal packed with protein. Lentils, on top of being incredibly versatile, are also an amazing budget saver. This version is flavored with Mediterranean spices that make a velvety smooth soup that's rich and flavorful. Have a bowl or two . . . or three.

Serves 4

$2.02 per serving

1 tbsp (15 ml) canola oil

1 medium-sized onion, diced

2 cloves garlic, minced

½ tsp ground cumin

½ tsp ground coriander

½ tsp dried parsley

¼ tsp sugar

1 tsp ground turmeric

3 cups (710 ml) vegetable broth or water

1 tsp salt

½ tsp freshly ground black pepper

1 cup (192 g) dried red lentils

Juice of ½ lemon

Fresh parsley, for garnish

Turn the pot to sauté mode on HIGH until the screen says hot. Add the oil, then the onion, and cook for 7 to 10 minutes, or until starting to brown. Add the garlic, cumin, coriander, parsley, sugar and turmeric, and cook for 1 minute. Stir in the broth, salt, pepper and lentils. Turn the pot to HIGH pressure, secure the lid, adjust the valve to sealing and set the timer for 45 minutes. When the time is up, do a quick release by turning the valve to venting. Once finished, release the lid.

Stir in the lemon juice and serve topped with parsley.

Navy Bean Soup

Protein packed and a great meal any night of the week. Only in an Instant Pot can you start with dried beans and end with a flavorful and perfectly textured bean soup. The flavorful broth is infused into every bean as they cook, delivering the ultimate flavor—you won't find that using canned beans.

Serves 6

$1.15 **per serving**

2 tbsp (30 ml) canola oil

1 medium-sized onion, diced

2 celery ribs, diced

2 medium-sized carrots, diced

4 cloves garlic, minced

1 lb (455 g) dried navy beans

2 (32-oz [946-ml]) containers vegetable broth

½ tsp dried thyme

1 bay leaf

½ tsp crushed red pepper flakes

1 tsp salt

Turn the pot to sauté mode on HIGH until the screen says hot. Add the oil, then the onion, celery and carrots, and cook for 5 to 7 minutes, or until softened. Stir in the garlic and cook for 1 minute.

Stir in the beans, vegetable broth, thyme, bay leaf, crushed red pepper flakes and salt. Turn the pot to HIGH pressure, secure the lid, adjust the valve to sealing and set the timer for 1 hour. When the time is up, do a quick release by turning the valve to venting. Once finished, release the lid and remove the bay leaf.

Transfer half of the soup to a blender; cover the blender with a towel or close and leave the easy-pour spout open, for the steam to escape. Blend until smooth. Return the blended soup back to the pot and stir.

Vegetarian Burrito Bowl

Load it up in a burrito or tacos; this mixture is a great meat substitute in any of your favorite Mexican recipes. But it's also great on its own, served in a bowl, topped with your favorite toppings, for a delicious vegetarian burrito bowl.

Serves 4

$2.08 per serving

1 tbsp (15 ml) canola oil

1 small red onion, diced

1 green bell pepper, seeded and diced

1 tsp ground cumin

1 cup (173 g) uncooked quinoa, rinsed well

1 cup (260 g) salsa

½ tsp salt

1½ cups (355 ml) water

1 (15.5-oz [439-g]) can black beans, drained and rinsed

Tortillas, for serving (optional)

Optional Toppings

Avocado

Guacamole

Fresh cilantro

Green onions

Salsa

Lime wedges

Shredded lettuce

Turn the pot to sauté mode on HIGH until the screen says hot. Add the oil, then the red onion and bell pepper, and cook for 6 to 8 minutes, or until the pepper is softened. Stir in the cumin and cook for 1 minute. Stir in the quinoa, salsa, salt, water and beans. Turn the pot to HIGH pressure, secure the lid, adjust the valve to sealing and set the timer for 12 minutes. When the time is up, do a quick release by turning the valve to venting. Once finished, release the lid.

Fluff the mixture before serving in bowls or on tortillas (if using) topped with your toppings of choice.

Cheesy Cauliflower Bake

The perfect low-carb mac and cheese substitute when you're looking for a little comfort without the guilt. Tender cauliflower is smothered in a delicious cheese sauce that's lighter than the original but packs in all of the flavor.

Serves 6

$1.76 per serving

1 cup (240 ml) water

2 heads cauliflower, cut into small florets

1 cup (240 ml) half-and-half

4 tbsp (60 g) cream cheese, at room temperature

1 tsp salt

½ tsp freshly ground black pepper

1½ cups (173 g) shredded sharp Cheddar cheese, divided

½ cup (60 g) breadcrumbs

Pour the water into the Instant Pot. Place the steamer basket in the pot. Add the cauliflower to the basket. Turn the pot to HIGH pressure, secure the lid, adjust the valve to sealing and set the timer for 10 minutes. When the time is up, do a quick release by turning the valve to venting. Once finished, release the lid.

Meanwhile, in a small pan over medium heat, heat the half-and-half until it begins to simmer. Stir in the cream cheese, salt, pepper and 1 cup (115 g) of the shredded Cheddar. Stir constantly until melted.

Remove the steamer basket and drain the water from the pot. Return the cauliflower to the pot. Add the cheese sauce and stir.

Set the oven to broil on HIGH. Add the cauliflower mixture to a 9 x 13–inch (23 x 33–cm) baking dish and top with the remaining ½ cup (58 g) of shredded cheese and the breadcrumbs. Broil for 3 to 5 minutes, or until the cheese is melted and bubbly.

Simple Ratatouille Bowls

Ratatouille is usually baked over a long period of time to result in its famous flavor, but this version comes together in less time, and you won't sacrifice anything for it! The vegetables cook along with the spices, which results in a decadent flavor that you will swear came from a fancy restaurant.

Serves 6

$2.39 per serving

2 tbsp (30 ml) canola oil

1 medium-sized onion, diced

6 cloves garlic, minced

2 zucchini, cut into ¼" (6-mm) pieces

1 large eggplant, cut into ¼" (6-mm) pieces

1 red bell pepper, seeded and cut into ½" (1.3-cm) pieces

1 green bell pepper, seeded and cut into ½" (1.3-cm) pieces

1 (15.5-oz [439-g]) can cannellini beans, drained

1 tsp salt

½ tsp freshly ground black pepper

1 tsp dried oregano

1 rosemary sprig

3 large tomatoes, cut into 1" (2.5-cm) pieces

5 fresh basil leaves, thinly sliced

1 tbsp (15 ml) balsamic vinegar, plus more for serving

1 tbsp (4 g) chopped parsley

Olive oil, for serving

Turn the pot to sauté mode on HIGH until the screen says hot. Add the oil, then the onion, and cook for 3 minutes or until translucent. Add the garlic and cook for 1 minute. Add the zucchini, eggplant and bell peppers, and cook for 3 to 5 minutes. Stir in the beans, salt, black pepper, oregano, rosemary and tomatoes. Turn the pot to HIGH pressure, secure the lid, adjust the valve to sealing and set the timer for 10 minutes. When the time is up, do a quick release by turning the valve to venting. Once finished, release the lid.

Remove the rosemary sprig and stir in the basil and balsamic vinegar until the basil is just wilted. Serve topped with the parsley, a drizzle of oil and balsamic vinegar.

Indian Curried Rice with Vegetables

Bound to be remembered for its bright yellow hue, this curried rice is loaded with flavor and is hardly any effort to make. With its tender vegetables, this makes for a great meal or side dish.

Serves 6

$1.86 per serving

1 tbsp (15 ml) canola oil
1 small onion, diced
2 cloves garlic, minced
2 carrots, diced
1 tsp salt
2 tsp (4 g) curry powder
1 cup (130 g) frozen peas
1 (14.5-oz [429-ml]) can chicken broth
1½ cups (293 g) uncooked basmati rice

Turn the pot to sauté mode on HIGH until the screen says hot. Add the oil, then the onion, and cook for 2 minutes, or until the edges begin to turn translucent. Add the garlic and cook for 1 minute. Stir in the carrots, salt, curry powder, peas and broth. Pour the rice on top. Turn the pot to HIGH pressure, secure the lid, adjust the valve to sealing and set the timer for 15 minutes. When the time is up, do a quick release by turning the valve to venting. Once finished, release the lid.

Fluff the rice before serving.

About the Author

Drew Maresco is the author of *3-Step Slow Cooker Cookbook* and the founder of the popular website BestRecipes.co and its magazine and book publications. He is a self-taught cook with a mind for creating unique and delicious recipes. His inspiration began at a young age while sitting on his grandmother's countertop as she let him assist with everything she baked. From there, he flourished into a dreamer and a foodie with goals for both. He became the owner of his first business at age nineteen, expanding from there to create his first food blog, which developed into what is now the ever-growing website and publication he presently runs. He has a real knack for taking a few simple ingredients and turning them into something unique and exceptional for all to enjoy. He has also had recipes published in various local magazines.

Drew was born and raised in the Detroit area of Michigan, which made for expanding his culinary palate. The large array of cultures that surround this area are an inspiration for him to try the foods from these cultures and learn cooking styles from their background and heritage. Enjoying new food and drinks everywhere he goes is a simple delight for him, making every day a new food adventure with deciding what new places to try.

Acknowledgments

Thank you to all of my friends and family who have been such a huge support in the production of this book. A special thank-you to the family members who ate all of the food while in the testing phase, and for all of the brutal honesty they gave me no matter what. Without that support, this book wouldn't be as great as it is.

Thank you, Marissa Giambelluca and Page Street Publishing, for taking this journey with me for a second time.

Index